West Academic Publishing's Law School Advisory Board

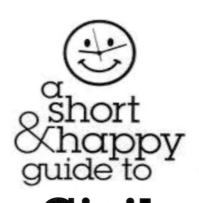

Civil
Procedure

by

Richard D. Freer
Robert Howell Hall Professor of Law,
Emory University

SHORT AND HAPPY SERIES™

WEST
ACADEMIC
PUBLISHING

Mat #41405748

© 2014 LEG, Inc. d/b/a West Academic

    444 Cedar Street, Suite 700
    St. Paul, MN 55101
    1-877-888-1330

Printed in the United States of America

ISBN: 978-0-314-28727-4

To Weasie, Collin, Courtney, Bee, Cookie, and Cheeto

Acknowledgments

I am delighted that Paula Franzese had the idea for the Short and Happy series. I am grateful to Louis Higgins at West Academic for allowing me to contribute this volume. Collin Freer and Lee Strasburger provided very useful advice and feedback, which I appreciate greatly. I am grateful to Sierra Sterling and Allison Midei, Emory Law class of 2014, for editorial suggestions.

Atlanta
May 2014

Table of Contents

ACKNOWLEDGMENTS.. V

Introduction. Why and How Law School Is Different from
    College..1

Chapter 1. The Study of Civil Procedure........................7
A. What Civil Procedure Is About 7
B. Some Background... 12

Chapter 2. Selecting a Forum: Personal Jurisdiction and
    Notice... 17
A. Overview and Terminology 17
B. Constitutional Limits on *In Personam* Jurisdiction........ 20
    From *Pennoyer* to *International Shoe* ("*Shoe*") 20
    Interpreting *Shoe*: From Fairness to the Importance
      of Contact 25
    Quick Recap 29
    Stream-of-Commerce.. 29
    "Effects" Jurisdiction 32
    Jurisdiction Based on Presence 33
    General and Specific Jurisdiction 34
    What About the Internet?................................... 36
C. Statutory Provisions for *In Personam* Jurisdiction 36
D. *In Rem* and *Quasi-in-Rem* Jurisdiction.................. 40
E. Approach for the Exam 43
    1. Statute... 43
    2. Constitution... 44
F. Notice and Opportunity to Be Heard........................ 47
    Service on a Human Defendant (A "Natural Person") ... 48
    Service on a Business 50
    Waiver of Service by Mail 50
    Geographic Limit 51

Chapter 3. Selecting a Forum: Subject Matter
    Jurisdiction 53
A. Overview 53
B. Diversity of Citizenship Jurisdiction..................... 54
    First Requirement: Citizens of Different States (The
      Complete Diversity Rule) 55
      Citizenship of a Natural Person........................ 56
      Citizenship of a Corporation 58
      Citizenship of Unincorporated Businesses 59

Second Requirement: Amount in Controversy 60
C.   Federal Question Jurisdiction 62
D.   Supplemental Jurisdiction 64
E.   Removal from State to Federal Court...................... 68

Chapter 4. Selecting a Forum: Venue, Transfer, and
Forum Non Conveniens....................................... **75**
A.   The General Venue Provisions.............................. 75
Residential Venue 77
Transactional Venue 78
"Fallback" Venue 78
B.   Transfer of Venue 79
The Federal Transfer Statutes 80
The Transferee District 81
Personal Jurisdiction in the Transferor Court....... 81
Choice of Law Issues................................... 81
C.   *Forum Non Conveniens* 83

Chapter 5. The Litigation Process: Early Stages............. 85
A.   Pleadings and Motions 85
The Complaint 85
Defendant's Response 88
Rule 11 91
Next Stages.. 91
B.   Discovery.. 91
Discovery Tools 92
Scope of Discovery 95
Enforcing the Discovery Provisions.......................... 98
C.   Pretrial Dismissal and Default.............................. 99

Chapter 6. The Litigation Process: Adjudication........... 101
A.   Overview... 101
B.   Adjudication Without Trial: Summary Judgment 101
C.   Adjudication at Trial.. 106
Jury Trial 106
The Difference Between Verdict and Judgment......... 110
D.   Motions for JMOL, RJMOL, and New Trial 111

Chapter 7. The Litigation Process: Appellate Review..... 117
A.   The Nature of Appellate Review............................ 117
B.   The Final Judgment Rule..................................... 118
C.   Interlocutory Review... 120
Statutory Provisions... 120

Federal Rules Provisions 120
Common Law... 121
Extraordinary Writ 122

**Chapter 8. Defining the Scope of Litigation: Joinder of
Claims and Parties 125**
A.   Permissive Party Joinder ("Proper Parties") 126
B.   Claim Joinder by Plaintiff................................ 128
C.   Claim Joinder by Defendant............................... 129
D.   Necessary (Required) and "Indispensable" Parties...... 132
E.   Impleader, or Third-Party Practice 136
F.   Intervention 137
G.   The Class Action 139
     Overview... 139
     Prerequisites 139
     Types of Class Action 141
     Settlement 142
     Subject Matter Jurisdiction 143

Chapter 9. The Preclusion Doctrines 145
A.   Overview and Terminology 145
B.   Claim Preclusion... 146
     Valid, Final Judgment on the Merits...................... 146
     Same Claimant Versus Same Defendant in Both
          Cases 148
     Claimant Asserted the Same Claim in Both Cases 149
C.   Issue Preclusion... 150
     Same Issue Litigated and Determined in Case 1 151
     That Issue Was Essential to the Judgment in Case 1.... 151
     Due Process: Against Whom Issue Preclusion May Be
          Asserted 152
     Mutuality: By Whom Issue Preclusion May Be
          Asserted 153

Chapter 10. *Erie*... 157
A.   *Swift* and *Erie*.. 157
B.   A Variety of Tests 160
C.   Two Doctrines, Not One 163
D.   Two Illustrative Hypos 165

TABLE OF CASES.. 169

A Short & Happy Guide to
Civil Procedure

Why and How Law School Is Different from College

Welcome to law school and welcome to Civil Procedure! Law school is exciting and intellectually stimulating. It is a pathway to many careers. But everyone seems to have a story about how tough law school can be. I think we should focus instead on something productive: it is helpful to understand (1) why and (2) how law school is different from college. Your goal here—your "job" as a law student—is different from what it was in college.

Why is law school different? Here, you are being educated and trained to practice a *profession*. That was not true in college. The goal of a liberal arts college education was to learn things for their intrinsic value, and not to apply them to any particular purpose.[1] Very few people make a living by knowing what Thucydides said about the Peloponnesian War or how to solve derivatives in calculus. You learned those things to discipline your

---

[1] Of course, not everyone gets a liberal arts education. Those with undergraduate degrees in engineering, for example, learn tools to be applied in a profession. Still, most law students were liberal arts majors. No matter your major, this section should help you adapt to law school.

1

mind and expand your horizons. Because what we studied in college was largely an end in itself, the goal of college exams and other assessment tools was to see whether we had learned the material.

Law school is different. Yes—you must know the material. You need to know the difference between *in personam* and *in rem* jurisdiction (and wow is that fun) and lots of other things. But you will not be assessed directly on whether you know these things. Instead, you will be assessed on how well you *apply* what you have learned to solve a problem raised by a fact pattern.

This reflects what you will do as a lawyer. No matter what area of law practice you pursue, clients will retain you to do one thing: to solve problems. Law is a problem-solving profession, and everything about law school is tied to that fact. The law we learn in class *is not an end in itself*. Rather, it is a tool with which to solve problems posed on the exam (just as it will be a tool with which to solve problems in the practice).

How is law school different from college? There are two major ways. First is the material we study. In college, we often read "textbooks" that synthesized fields of study. In law school, we do not assign "textbooks." We assign "casebooks." They are not full of textual explication and synthesis. They are full of *raw materials*. In most courses, the chief raw material will be cases. By "cases" we mean judicial decisions ruling on real-world disputes. The court's decision is laid out in the judge's opinion, which details her reasoning in reaching her conclusion. You will want to discern the court's "holding," which is the legal principle established in the case. There are other raw materials too, such as the Constitution, statutes, regulations and rules (like the Federal Rules of Civil Procedure).

So, for example, you will learn the law of Torts not by discussing a text that synthesizes the cases and tells you "the elements of the tort of battery are X, Y, and Z." Instead, you will study the opinions in which the judges determined that the elements of battery are X, Y, and Z. In Civil Procedure, you will learn what supplemental jurisdiction is not because some text tells you but because you pore through statutory language and cases interpreting that language.

This method of learning can be frustrating. Everyone struggles to figure out what the court's rationale is and how to summarize its reasoning. So why do we do it this way? After all, there *are* books that synthesize and summarize the law (indeed, this little volume is one). If all we wanted to know was the present state of the law, reading textual summaries would be fine. But we would not be good lawyers. We would not see how the law develops over time. We would not be adept at determining what should happen when a client's situation is slightly different from the facts presented in the reported cases. Lawyers must be able to roll up their sleeves and wrestle with the raw materials and reason to a conclusion. This process starts in law school.

The second major way in which law school differs from college is the way we grade. In college, we had quizzes and midterms and papers and projects and final exams. The grade was usually based on some combination of these. In law school, we tend to base the entire grade on the final exam. This is tough; it means there is no feedback until it is too late for the feedback to do any good. It's a Pepto-Bismol moment. But take heart— everybody is in the same boat! This is new for everyone.

More to the point, though, there is a lot you can do to be ready for exams. Throughout this book, I have pointers geared toward getting you ready for the Civil Procedure exam. One example is in Chapter 2, § E, where we propose an analytical approach that (IMHO) will handle any personal jurisdiction essay question.

But let's start with a tip that should help you in every course. Some professors might not put it this bluntly, but I think almost all would agree with the sentiment: on exams you get zero credit for demonstrating that you know what the law is. Let that sink in for a moment. This is different from college, where you were showing your professor that you had learned the stuff. Here, it is not enough to *know* the stuff. Here, you must *apply* the material to solve a problem. *Every point you ever earn on a law school exam will be from applying the facts to that law to solve a problem.*

So relax about the law—it will take a good deal of work, but you will know the law. The exam is about recognizing *facts* that apply to the law. For example, in Chapter 3, § B, we will discuss (among other things) the concept of "domicile." Every human has a domicile, and can only have one at a time. It is your "official" or "permanent" home.

Let's say that Courtney is domiciled in Georgia, and the question is whether she has changed her domicile to California. It takes two things to change your domicile: (1) physically, you must go to the new state and (2) mentally, you must form the intent to make that state your permanent home. (Some courts say it a bit differently, but all agree there is a physical requirement and a mental requirement.)

We can figure out a lot about the exam even now. Of those two requirements, which is going to be a big deal on the exam? The requirement of physical presence simply cannot be difficult— either Courtney is in California or she is not. But the question of her intent is eminently testable. Think about why. Few people wake up one day and say "hey, I have formed the intent to make this state my permanent home." Usually, the formation of intent is gradual; people move to a new state and try it out, and at some point it becomes clear this is their new domicile. Knowing that the intent issue is readily testable, be aggressive. Go into the exam looking for *facts* that show that the person is putting down permanent roots.

> Example: Courtney accepts a job in California and moves there. After six months, she is promoted to a management position and the boss says "we look forward to a long career for you here." Courtney buys a house in California. She pays California real estate, income, and other taxes. She joins a church and a civic club in California. She registers to vote there. She registers her car there. She gets a California driver's license. She qualifies for instate tuition at a state university.

On the exam, if we asked "what is the definition of domicile," everyone would get a perfect score. But we never ask that question. Why? Because in the history of the world, no client has ever run into a lawyer's office and said: "Tell me, I gotta know—what is the definition of domicile?" Instead, the client tells you a story—a fact pattern. And you have to figure out what facts are relevant. That's exactly what a law school exam is—a fact pattern. And we have to figure out what facts are relevant.

In the Example above, at least ten facts support the conclusion that Courtney has formed an intent to make California her permanent home. On the exam, they would not be so easy to spot, because they would not be listed together; they would be sprinkled throughout the fact pattern. On an exam with these facts, almost all students would recount at least three of the facts in their discussion of domicile. The average answer might get five or six of the facts. Someone who recounted eight of the facts would get a higher grade than someone who discussed six. *That* is where the grade is determined—applying facts to the law.

And here's another reason to relax: over the course of an exam, nobody comes anywhere near getting all the possible points. So have fun with it—it's a scavenger hunt for the facts.

Enough about exams! Now, let's cut to the chase: why is Civil Procedure the best first-year class?

CHAPTER 1

The Study of Civil Procedure

A. What Civil Procedure Is About

When you looked at the list of courses for the first year of law school, you saw a lot of familiar subjects. Contracts? You've signed contracts with your cellphone company and to lease your apartment and to buy your car. In fact, when you were a kid, you may have had a deal with your parents: if you did your chores, you were paid an allowance. That was a contract. So we all know something about Contracts. Property? Everybody knows something about that—at least, everybody who has had a roommate. Torts? Well, nobody knows that word, but once you get into it, it's no mystery. It comes as no surprise that if you drive your car negligently and injure someone, you can be sued. Criminal Law? Everybody knows something about that, though hopefully only from TV and movies.

But Civil Procedure? There is no family—no matter how dysfunctional—that sits around talking about venue and claim preclusion and the *Erie* doctrine. So the mystery about Civil Procedure comes from the fact that we have never seen it before.

Civil Procedure is about *litigation,* which is a publicly-funded method for resolving disputes. It is where we "go to court" to resolve our differences with others. We are concerned with *civil* litigation.[2] In a civil case, the plaintiff (P) sues the defendant (D) to seek recovery for harm inflicted on her by D. Often, P sues for *damages*—that is, money to compensate P. Sometimes the remedy is not monetary. For example, P may want the court to issue an injunction forbidding D from trespassing on her property.

In "substantive" courses like Contracts, Torts, and Property, you learn the rules by which society lives. You learn about the rights that we may enforce through litigation. In Civil Procedure, we learn the *rules by which those substantive rights are enforced.* The procedural rules are "trans-substantive," which means that we use the same procedure for all cases. If you are going to be a civil litigator, Civil Procedure may be the most important real-world course in your first year of law school. Even if you do not intend to litigate—if, for instance, you want to help clients plan their business or estate or tax matters—it is helpful to know how your clients' rights may be vindicated through litigation if the planning results in a dispute.

In the United States, we adopt the "adversarial system" of justice. The idea is that each side, represented by lawyers, puts on her case as strongly as possible. We believe that this conflict, with each party challenging the other's presentation through cross-examination of witnesses, holds the greatest promise for discerning the truth and reaching a just resolution. This is quite different from the "inquisitorial system" used in most of continental Europe, in which the court is largely responsible for running the show and directing the gathering of evidence. Movies

---

[2]   We are *not* concerned with criminal litigation, in which the government (state or federal) prosecutes a defendant for allegedly violating the criminal law. If the defendant is convicted, she may be sentenced to jail time or to community service, or ordered to pay a fine.

and TV about American litigation often give the impression that P files a case against D and then, some short time later, P and D show up at a trial in the courtroom and tell their respective stories to the jury. This is an inaccurate view (except in small claims cases). The litigation process is substantially longer than most people realize—often measured in years rather than months. What are the litigants, lawyers, and the court doing during that time?

Before P even files the case, her lawyer must select an appropriate court in which to sue. "Forum selection" implicates three major units of the Civil Procedure course: personal jurisdiction, subject matter jurisdiction, and venue. Once the case is filed, D may contest the selection of forum, the parties will argue the matter in briefs, and the court will rule.

To get an idea of why forum selection matters, consider a hypothetical. Suppose you are a citizen of State A. You go on vacation to Hawaii, to the island of Maui. There, you drive on the famous (but curvy) Hana Highway. You collide with Other Driver (OD), who is a citizen of State Z. You want to sue OD to recover damages for the harm you suffered from the collision. And OD wants to sue you.

Where do you sue? You would like to sue in State A. After all, that is your home, so suing there means (1) you will not have to travel, (2) your lawyer can represent you, and (3) you have a hunch that a State A judge and jury might be favor you over OD. For the same reasons, OD wants to sue you in State Z. This presents the issue of *personal jurisdiction*—in which state does the litigation proceed? In Chapter 2 we will learn that one has a due process right to be sued only in states with which she has formed some volitional contact. So maybe you cannot sue OD in State A (and maybe she cannot sue you in State Z). Then what? Either of you could sue the other in Hawaii. You and OD certainly have volitional ties there, and the claims arose there.

Let's say, though, that you *are* subject to personal jurisdiction in State Z and that OD sues you there. Now we address *subject matter jurisdiction*, which we study in Chapter 3. In every state, there are two sets of courts: state courts and federal courts. Assume that OD's case against you could be heard by either a state or federal court. OD will probably choose to go to state court. This is because most state-court judges are elected. OD will want to litigate before a judge whose career is in the hands of local voters (after all, OD is a local voter). Not only that, but the jury in state court is drawn from a small area, usually a county. Local jurors might favor the local person. You, on the other hand, will prefer federal court. Federal judges are appointed for life and never face an election, so a federal judge could rule in your favor without fear of reprisal from the local voters. Plus, the federal jury is drawn from a much larger geographic area, and might be less parochial.

As we see with this example, there is a great deal to consider in simply selecting the right court. And there is a third forum-selection hurdle, called venue, which we address in Chapter 4.

After P's lawyer determines the forum in which to sue, she can file the case and start the litigation process. In Chapter 5 we address the early stages, which consist of filing "pleadings" and "motions" and, if the case is not dismissed, "discovery." Discovery is a process by which each party may demand that the other party surrender information relevant to the case. At some point, the case may become ripe for adjudication, perhaps in trial (perhaps by jury) or maybe by something called "summary judgment." Surprisingly few cases actually go to trial. In federal courts, of all cases filed, *fewer than two percent* will go to trial. The vast majority will be resolved on motion or by settlement, so trial is not necessary. Once the trial court disposes of the case, the losing party may seek appellate review, which we discuss in Chapter 7.

At that point, we will have taken a simple case from forum selection through judgment and appeal. In Chapter 8, we explore the possibility of joining multiple parties or claims in a single case, which may make the case more complex but more efficient. In Chapter 9, we look at the possibility that a judgment entered in our case may preclude us (or others) from litigating in another case. Finally, in Chapter 10, we talk about the *Erie* doctrine, which raises important issues of federalism—the allocation of authority between the federal and state governments. Specifically, *Erie* concerns when a federal court must apply state law.

There is no single "right" order in which to cover these topics. Many courses follow the order we adopt in this book, but many do not. That does not matter. This book will help you fit the pieces together no matter the order of presentation. Of course, you should emphasize the topics your professor emphasizes. Moreover, there are some areas of Civil Procedure in which professors can take quite differing views. Examples are some aspects of personal jurisdiction and the *Erie* doctrine. With these topics especially, it is a good idea to know your professor's thoughts on the matter.

Civil Procedure offers a remarkable mix of types of material. Some of the things we study are mechanical—the rules are clear and usually yield a definite answer. But other parts of the course are extremely amorphous—the courts have given us some factors to apply but it is not clear how much each factor matters or what the ultimate answer will be. *Use the different types of material to your advantage.* When we deal with mechanical rules (for example, service of process and discovery), you simply must memorize some detailed rules and apply them. But in the amorphous areas (and the best example is personal jurisdiction), free yourself from the burden of trying to find the "right" answer. There is no "right" answer on such topics. On these, you need to walk your professor through the relevant factors, apply the facts to them, and come to a reasonable conclusion.

B. Some Background

Here we will discuss some background matters that will set the stage for our course. First, we should know something about the structure of a judicial system. Every state has its own court system, and is free to set it up as it sees fit. In addition, there is a completely separate federal court system. So there are 51 separate court systems in this country (actually more than that, because non-states such as the District of Columbia and Puerto Rico have local court systems as well). Throughout the book, we will occasionally refer to practice in state courts, but will focus on the federal judicial system and the Federal Rules of Civil Procedure, which apply in federal court. We will refer to specific provisions of the Federal Rules of Civil Procedure as "Rule" or "FRCP."

The lowest level court in any judicial system is the "trial court." In the federal judiciary, the trial court is the "federal district court." (States use various names for their trial courts, such as superior court or district court or any of a half dozen others.) Most of what we cover in Civil Procedure takes place in the trial court. This is where we worry about forum selection, pleadings, discovery, and adjudication. This is where we have trials and juries. In federal district court, a single judge is in charge of the case throughout the trial-court proceedings.

After the trial court resolves the case, the loser may seek review by a "higher" court. In the federal system, there is an intermediate appellate court, the United States Court of Appeals, to which there is a statutory right to appeal adverse judgments from the district court. The U.S. Court of Appeals is divided into "circuits" mostly along geographic lines. For example, the U.S.

Court of Appeals for the Eleventh Circuit, which "sits" in Atlanta, hears appeals from district courts in Florida, Georgia, and Alabama.

Appellate courts review decisions of the trial court "on the record," which means that they review the file from the trial court, including the transcript of testimony at a trial. Appellate courts do not hold evidentiary hearings. There is no discovery. There is no jury. Each side files briefs arguing the merits of the appeal and makes oral argument (usually 30 minutes per side) before a "panel" of judges. The panel is assigned at random from the membership of the appellate court and usually consists of three judges. The appeal of a final judgment from district court to the U.S. Court of Appeals ordinarily will take months, routinely over a year. (In some state systems, there is no intermediate court of appeals; when there is, its function usually is the same as the federal court of appeals.)

At the top of the system is the "court of last resort." In the federal system, of course, this is the Supreme Court of the United States, which consists of nine justices and hears cases only in Washington, D.C. It is an appellate court, so it reviews the case on the record. Instead of hearing cases in panels, however, the entire Court usually participates in the decision of each case. The Supreme Court's jurisdiction is discretionary. It hears only the cases it decides to hear (which it does by granting a writ of *certiorari*). In a typical year, the Court is asked to review over 7500 cases. It will actually hold oral argument and render an opinion in about 80. (Each state has a court of last resort, which usually exercises discretionary review in civil cases.)

Though the United States Court of Appeals and Supreme Court exercise appellate jurisdiction, they play different roles. The Court of Appeals reviews the trial court proceedings to determine whether that court committed reversible error. This function polices whether the trial judge applied law properly in resolving the case. The Supreme Court, however, is less concerned with policing the trial court than with providing clarity in the law, often by resolving legal issues on which lower courts have reached different conclusions.

As a general rule, once a case is in one judicial system—state or federal—it stays there. If the case is decided in a state trial court, the appeal must go up the state-court system, to the state court of appeals (if there is one) and to the state high court (if it will hear the case). One cannot appeal from a state trial court to a federal appellate court. Federal courts do not sit in judgment of what state courts do. States and the federal government are separate sovereigns. There is one exception to this, however: the Supreme Court (when that phrase is capitalized, we are talking about the Supreme Court of the United States) can review decisions from the highest state court, *but only* on matters of federal law. If the question is whether State X enforces certain types of contracts, the highest court of State X is the ultimate arbiter. No federal court can tell that court what State X law should be. But if the question is whether the supreme court of State X misinterpreted or violated some federal law in its ruling, the Supreme Court may review, but only on that federal issue.

Finally, let's talk about enforcement of a judgment. Suppose P wins a case and has a judgment against D for $100,000. D might write a check to P and the judgment will be discharged. What if D does not do this? If the judgment was *in personam* (which, as we see in the next chapter, the court had power over D herself and not her property), it creates a personal obligation for D to pay P. Let's say P won the judgment in California. If D has property in California (any kind of property—a house, a bank account, a car, a library of Pilates CDs),[3] a court can enforce the judgment by directing the sheriff to seize D's property and sell it at public auction to raise money to pay the judgment. If the sale fetches more than $100,000, P gets her $100,000 and D gets what's left. What if the sale fetches $70,000? P gets the $70,000. But D still owes her $30,000. The judgment is still valid to that extent. If P finds that D has property in Maine, P can go to a court in Maine and have it enforce the judgment by directing the sheriff to seize it and sell it.

Why is the California judgment enforceable in Maine? The full faith and credit clause of the Constitution requires each state to enforce the valid judgments of sister states. The key word is "valid." A valid judgment is one entered by a court that had both personal jurisdiction and subject matter jurisdiction. So we need to know how a court can get personal jurisdiction and subject matter jurisdiction. Luckily, those are the subjects of the next two chapters.

---

[3]   In Chapter 2, § D, we will see that the D's property can be the basis of jurisdiction itself. Such cases are *in rem* or *quasi-in-rem*. That is not what we are talking about here. Here we had *in personam* jurisdiction over D (that is jurisdiction over D, not over her property), P has won a judgment and is trying to collect on the judgment.

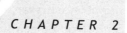

CHAPTER 2

Selecting a Forum: Personal Jurisdiction and Notice

A. Overview and Terminology

The court in which we litigate is an arm of the government, either state or federal. The court will issue orders to the parties and may ultimately enter a judgment determining the rights of the parties. No court may issue binding orders to people or determine their rights unless it has authority to do so. The government (state or federal) must have legitimate bases on which to affect someone's rights.

In the law, we say that the court must have *jurisdiction*. There are two kinds of jurisdiction (we mentioned them in Chapter 1, § A). First, the court must have jurisdiction over the parties, or "personal jurisdiction." Second, it must also have jurisdiction over the case itself—in other words, it must be empowered to decide this kind of dispute; this is "subject matter jurisdiction." Personal jurisdiction is exercised over *parties*. Subject matter jurisdiction is exercised over *cases*. A court that lacks jurisdiction of either type cannot legitimately affect anyone's rights. A judgment entered by a court that lacks either personal or subject matter jurisdiction is void.

For personal jurisdiction, courts historically spoke of having "power" over the parties. You have a constitutional right to be sued *only* in places that have such power over you. This right is waivable, however, and a person may consent to litigate before a court that otherwise would not have personal jurisdiction.[1] By filing the case, P automatically submits to personal jurisdiction. So the only question is whether the court will have personal jurisdiction over the defendant (D).

Personal jurisdiction is exercised on a state-by-state basis (even if we are going to a federal court). So the question of personal jurisdiction is one of geography: can P sue D in this state? The answer to the question will be the same in federal court as in state court. That is, a federal court in California can exercise personal jurisdiction over a defendant only if a state court in California could do so. (Suppose California does have personal jurisdiction. The *next* jurisdictional question is whether the case will proceed in a state court in California or in a federal court in California. That is the question of subject matter jurisdiction.)

To have personal jurisdiction, the court must have authority (or power) over one of two things: either (1) over D herself or (2) over D's property. Stated in fancier terms, there are two possible "jurisdictional predicates," and the court must have power over at least one of them: D's person or D's property. The jurisdictional predicate affects our terminology. There are three types of personal jurisdiction: (1) *in personam*, (2) *in rem*, and (3) *quasi-in-rem*. With *in personam*, the court has power over D herself. With

---

[1]   We will see in Chapter 3 that subject matter jurisdiction is different. The court must have subject matter jurisdiction (authority over the particular type of case) independent of waiver by the parties. In fact, the parties cannot waive restrictions on subject matter jurisdiction.

the other two, the court has power over D's property. This makes sense. "Personam" is Latin for "person" and "rem" is from "res" (pronounced "race"), which means "thing."

P will always prefer to get *in personam* jurisdiction if she can. A valid *in personam* judgment creates a debt, a personal obligation, which can be enforced in any other state. Sometimes, however, P cannot get *in personam* jurisdiction. If D has property in the forum, she might be able to have the court seize that property and use the property as the jurisdictional predicate. A judgment *in rem* or *quasi in rem* does not create a personal obligation. Instead, it will determine the parties' rights in that property.

We said above that D has a *constitutional* right to be sued only in courts that have personal jurisdiction. Specifically, the protection is accorded by due process. The Fifth Amendment to the United States Constitution provides that the federal government may not deprive anyone of property without "due process of law." The Fourteenth Amendment says the same thing regarding state governments. We will see in § F that due process *also* requires that the court give D notice of the suit against her and an opportunity to be heard.

Focusing now on personal jurisdiction (and leaving notice until later), it is helpful to think of the due process clauses as establishing a large circle—the due process circle. If our case falls within that circle, the judgment is constitutionally valid. If the case falls outside that circle, however, the judgment is void. But (and this is as important as it may be surprising), the fact that our case falls within the due process circle does not automatically mean that the court has personal jurisdiction! There is another step. The state in which the court sits must have passed a statute that allows the court to exercise personal jurisdiction. Stated another way, personal jurisdiction is not self-executing. A court only gets to exercise personal jurisdiction if (1) a state statute says it's OK and (2) the exercise of personal jurisdiction comports with due process.

So analytically (in the real world and on your exam), the *first step* in determining whether the forum has personal jurisdiction is whether the forum state has a statute that allows the court to exercise personal jurisdiction. *If the answer to that question is yes* (or arguably yes), then we assess whether the case falls within the due process circle. Having said that, however, in this book we will take the topics in reverse order. We will discuss the constitutional limits first. Why? Because your course will undoubtedly devote far more time to this question than to the statutory question. Moreover, once we understand the constitutional limits on personal jurisdiction, the statutory material will be relatively easy.

B. Constitutional Limits on *In Personam* Jurisdiction

From Pennoyer *to* International Shoe *("Shoe")*

The due process clauses of the Fifth and Fourteenth Amendments give defendants a "liberty interest" that she cannot be sued in a state that does not have personal jurisdiction over her. To determine the due process limits, we must consider a series of Supreme Court decisions, starting with the iconic nineteenth-century case of *Pennoyer v. Neff*, 95 U.S. 714 (1878).

The point of this journey is *not* to enable you to write a history essay on your exam (unless your prof wants that). That is not your job. Your job is to apply the law *as it exists today* to a fact pattern that your professor gives you. But you cannot understand the law as it exists today without taking the journey. Here's the goal: for each case, we distill the principle (or principles) established. Later, in § E, we will pull all the principles together in an analytical framework that you can apply to any fact pattern on your exam. The cases we discuss may not match all the cases you read in your course. Don't worry about that—most of the cases will be on everyone's journey.

One more point before we start: *in personam* jurisdiction is either "specific" or "general." With general *in personam* jurisdiction, D can be sued in the forum on a claim that arose anywhere in the world. With specific *in personam* jurisdiction, D is sued in the forum for a claim that arose from her activities in the forum. So if D is subject to general jurisdiction in California, she can be sued there for a claim that arose in California or in New York or in Bolivia. If D is subject to specific jurisdiction in California, she can only be sued there on a claim that arose in California—for something she did in (or that caused an effect in) California. Though the Court has not used this term, many people refer to this topic as "relatedness," to capture the notion that we address whether P's claim is related to D's contact with the forum. If the claim arises from what D did in the forum, the court will have specific jurisdiction. If not, we must satisfy the requirements for general jurisdiction.

The starting point is *Pennoyer v. Neff*, which is one of the most famous cases ever decided. In *Pennoyer*, the Court spoke in terms of raw physical power: the state has power (and therefore jurisdiction) over persons and things found within the state boundaries. The Court does not discuss whether jurisdiction would be "fair" or "convenient." If the person or property is in the state, the state can exercise jurisdiction. When the power is over persons, the court has *in personam* jurisdiction. When the power is over property or things, it is *in rem* or *quasi-in-rem* jurisdiction.

Pennoyer established what are still called the "traditional bases" of *in personam* jurisdiction.[2] First, the court has jurisdiction if D is served with process in the forum.[3] We refer to this basis as "presence," but note, it is not met simply because D was present in the state at some point. She must have been present in the forum state when she was served with process. (Some people call this "tag" jurisdiction because we "tag" D with service of process while she is in the forum state.

Service on D instate gives the court general *in personam* jurisdiction, so D can be sued there on a claim that arose anywhere. (Instead of serving process directly on D, it is possible to serve D's agent in the forum—if she has one. This would require D to send someone into the state essentially representing her (maybe to do business there on her behalf).)

Second, the court has jurisdiction if D is domiciled in the forum. The Court spoke in terms of "residence," but it is clear that it meant domicile. We will define this term in Chapter 3, § B. Domicile also is a basis for general *in personam* jurisdiction.

Third, jurisdiction can be based upon consent. We saw in the preceding section that any D may waive an objection to personal jurisdiction. She might do so for all purposes and therefore be subject to general jurisdiction. Or she might do so for limited purposes and be subject to specific jurisdiction.

---

[2]　*Pennoyer* concerned the validity of the judgment in the previous case of Mitchell v. Neff, which was *QIR*, and not *in personam*. (See the discussion in § D.) So the Court's discussion of *in personam* jurisdiction in *Pennoyer* was dictum. Nonetheless, the Court later adopted it in in personam cases. Moreover, because *Mitchell v. Neff* was decided before promulgation of the Fourteenth Amendment, the holding in *Pennoyer* could not be based upon that provision's due process clause. It was, instead, based upon the full faith and credit provision. In practical terms, this also does not matter, because the Court later adopted the *Pennoyer* reasoning for due process analysis.

[3]　We will see in § F that service of process is the traditional way in which D is given notice that she has been sued. It requires that a process server deliver to D a summons, which is official notification from the court, and a copy of P's complaint.

Notice how difficult it is to get *in personam* jurisdiction under *Pennoyer*. At least one of the three bases (presence, consent, or domicile) must be satisfied. So unless D consents or is domiciled in the forum, the only way to sue her is to find her in the state and serve process on her there. This may not have been a problem in 1878, because people could not travel very easily or quickly. As society became more mobile, however, with the automobile and the airplane, it became much easier for a defendant to go to another state, commit a tort or breach a contract, and get out before being sued and served with process there. For half a century, the Court reacted to such change by expanding the application of the traditional bases.

The best example of this expansion is *Hess v. Pawloski*, 274 U.S. 352 (1927). There D, a citizen of Pennsylvania, drove his car to Massachusetts, where he was involved in a car wreck with P. P sued D in Massachusetts. By the time he did so, however, D had left Massachusetts and could not be served with process there. The Massachusetts "nonresident motorist statute" provided that by driving one's motor vehicle into Massachusetts, a nonresident (1) consents to *in personam* jurisdiction for a claim arising from operation of the vehicle and (2) appoints a state official as her agent for receiving service of process. The statute allows only specific jurisdiction—D can be sued in Massachusetts only for a claim arising from her operation of the vehicle there.

In *Hess*, the Supreme Court upheld jurisdiction. The opinion is brilliant because it adapts *Pennoyer* to a more mobile world. First, it expands the notion of consent to include implied consent. Just by driving over the state line, D consents to specific jurisdiction there.[4] Second, it expands the notion of service of process on D's

---

[4]   How can a state "coerce" your consent like this? After all, the privileges and immunities clause of the Constitution means, among other things, that one state cannot deny entry to the citizen of another state. But that does not prohibit a state from refusing to allow you to enter in a motor vehicle. Every state has a public

agent to include an agent appointed by operation of law. So service was made in the forum, as required by *Pennoyer*. Does *Hess* matter today? You bet—to this day, every state has a nonresident motorist act. Every time you drive across a state line you consent to specific *in personam* jurisdiction and appoint an agent for service of process.

By 1945, the time had come to restate principles underlying *in personam* jurisdiction. It is impossible to overstate the importance of *International Shoe Co. v. Washington*, 326 U.S. 310 (1945) *(Shoe)*, which was decided in that year. In *Shoe*, we do not find nineteenth-century language about raw physical power. Instead, we hear about "fairness," a "balance of convenience," and we see flexible analysis. *Shoe* gives us language with which courts are still wrestling: a state has *in personam* jurisdiction if D has "such minimum contacts with [the forum] that the maintenance of the suit does not offend traditional notions of fair play and substantial justice." You will know that phrase in your sleep (hopefully not while sleeping in class.) Let's make four points about *Shoe*.

- First, the language of *Shoe* is extremely imprecise. What are "minimum contacts"? What are "traditional notions of fair play"? What is "substantial justice"? This open-ended language will do two things: (1) lead to an expansion of jurisdiction and (2) make it difficult to predict when there will be jurisdiction on a given fact pattern. (It also opens the door for you to make arguments for and against jurisdiction on the exam!)

---

interest in ensuring safety on its roads. To do so, it has the right to infer your consent to suit simply by the fact that you drove into the state. So a state cannot keep you out altogether, but it can impose conditions on letting you in in a motor vehicle.

- Second, by the time the Court decided *Shoe*, it was clear that process could be served outside the forum state. In *Milliken v. Meyer*, 311 U.S. 457 (1940), the Court confirmed that one is subject to general jurisdiction in the state in which she is domiciled, and that if she happens to be outside that state when suit is filed, she can be served with process in another state. So now, with *Shoe*, it is clear that you need not have process served on D in the forum, so long as D has such contacts with the forum as to satisfy the *Shoe* test.

- Third, the quoted language from *Shoe* seems to consist of two parts: a contact part and a fairness part. (The Court will confirm this later.)

- Fourth, nowhere does the Court purport to overrule *Pennoyer*. Indeed, take a good look in your casebook at the phrase in the opinion immediately before the famous language we quoted above. The Court gives us that famous language as the test to be applied— get this—"if [the defendant] be not present in the forum." Read literally, this means that the *Shoe* test applies only when you cannot serve process on D in the forum. This implies that the *Pennoyer* traditional bases exist *alongside Shoe*, and that basing jurisdiction on *Shoe* is an *alternative* to basing it on one of the traditional bases. (We will see below that this issue is open to doubt.)

Interpreting Shoe*: From Fairness to the Importance of Contact*

For 12 years, the Court applied *Shoe* expansively by emphasizing "fairness." For instance, in *McGee v. International*

Life Ins. Co., 355 U.S. 220 (1957), an elderly California woman whose son died claimed to be the beneficiary of his life insurance policy. The insurer, a Texas company, rejected the claim, and the woman sued the Texas company in California. The Texas company had only sold one policy of insurance in California—the one at issue in the suit—so it did not have much contact with the forum. On the other hand, that contact resulted from the Texas company's soliciting business in California. The Court upheld jurisdiction, emphasizing the fairness of doing so. While it would be difficult for the woman to go to Texas to sue the company, the company could readily litigate in California. Also, California—as forum—had an interest in protecting its people from insurance fraud.

The following year, the Court took a radical turn. In *Hanson v. Denckla,* 357 U.S. 235 (1958), the Court started focusing less on fairness and the forum state's interest and more on whether D had established a sufficient contact with the forum. Under *Hanson,* contact between D and the forum must have been created by D's "purposeful availment" of the forum, meaning that D must have availed herself of benefits of the state. In *Hanson,* a wealthy Pennsylvania woman formed a trust fund with a Delaware bank. After several years, the woman moved to Florida, from which she continued to receive money from and send directions to the Delaware bank. After she died, her children sued each other in Florida about who inherited what. The Court held that Florida did not have jurisdiction over the Delaware bank. True, the bank had engaged in various transactions in Florida—but only because its client had moved there. The Delaware bank's contacts with Florida thus were reactive to what its client did. The bank did not itself reach out to Florida for some benefit. Thus it had no relevant contact with that state.

Twenty-two years later, in *World-Wide Volkswagen v. Woodson,* 444 U.S. 286 (1980), the Court reinforced the focus on defendant's volitional contact with the forum. There, a New York family bought a car in New York to drive to the new family home in Arizona. Tragically, they were rear-ended in Oklahoma, the car burst into flames, and family members suffered horrible injuries. They sued in Oklahoma, alleging that the car was defectively designed. Two defendants—the German manufacturer and the American importer for North America—did not contest jurisdiction. Two others—the regional distributor (which did business in New York, New Jersey, and Connecticut) and the retailer (which did business in New York) did contest jurisdiction. The Court held that the latter two could not be sued in Oklahoma. The reasoning was the same as in *Hanson*: the car sold by these two defendants ended up in Oklahoma, but those defendants did nothing to send it there. The car got there by the unilateral act of a third party (here, the plaintiffs, who drove the car to Oklahoma). Without purposeful availment *by the defendant of the forum* there can be no contact and thus no jurisdiction under *Shoe*.

One argument in the case was that it was "foreseeable" that a car sold in New York would get to Oklahoma. The Court said that foreseeability that the product may get into the forum is not enough. Instead, it must be foreseeable that D would be sued ("haled into court") there.[5]

The next big case is *Burger King Corp. v. Rudzewicz*, 471 U.S. 462 (1985), which involved a contract (rather than tort) claim. BK sued two Michigan men who ran a BK restaurant in Michigan. The suit was for alleged breach of various aspects of the agreement by which they were to run the restaurant. BK is headquartered in Miami, and filed suit there. The Court upheld jurisdiction and emphasized that *Shoe* consists of two parts: first, there must be a relevant contact and (if there is), second, the exercise of

---

[5]   Many people think this is circular. If we can foresee that a product will get into the forum, and we know that defective products can hurt people, isn't it therefore foreseeable that the defendant would get sued there?

⌐diction must be fair (or reasonable). Moreover, *there must be a relevant contact before fairness becomes relevant*. So even if the forum is the most convenient and fairest place for the litigation, it does not have jurisdiction unless D created a relevant contact with it.

On the facts in *Burger King*, there was no question about contact. The two Michigan franchisees purposefully availed themselves of Florida by reaching out to BK to enter a 20-year franchise relationship governed by Florida law. The big issue in *Burger King* was whether jurisdiction would be fair, or reasonable. In assessing this, the Court listed five "fairness factors" (the list came from *World-Wide*). The Court has never told us how to weigh these factors or which is most important. They are: (1) inconvenience for the defendant and her witnesses (in having to travel to the forum), (2) forum state's interest (we saw an example in *McGee*), (3) plaintiff's interest in litigating in the forum, (4) the legal system's interest in efficiency,[6] and (5) shared substantive policies of the states.[7]

The defendants argued that it was unfair for the big multinational plaintiff to drag them to Florida to litigate. They had relatively little money and BK had a lot of money. The Court, in an opinion by Justice Brennan, said, essentially, "tough luck—you can travel." Once we get to the fairness factors, the burden is on D to show that the forum is so "gravely" inconvenient that they are at a "severe disadvantage" in the litigation. This is nearly impossible to show, because, Brennan added, the relative wealth of the parties is not determinative. Thus, due process does not guarantee that D will be sued in the most convenient forum, or even a "good"

---

[6] If this were a big deal, it seems there should have been jurisdiction in *World-Wide*. Lack of jurisdiction over the regional distributor and the retailer meant that there might be multiple suits—one in Oklahoma and one in New York.

[7] The Court occasionally hints at such things. In *Kulko v. Superior Court*, 436 U.S. 84 (1978), it declined jurisdiction, saying that an interest in family harmony was furthered by refusing jurisdiction.

forum. It guarantees that she will not be sued in an unconstitutionally unfair forum.

Quick Recap

To this point, the Court seems to have shifted its analysis under *Shoe*. From *McGee*, which considered issues of contact and fairness and convenience in a mélange, we see the emergence of a two-part test. First, there must be a relevant contact between D and the forum. Without that contact, fairness factors are irrelevant! And the contact must be the result of D's purposeful availment of the forum. Second, if there is a relevant contact, D has the burden of showing—based upon five fairness factors—that the forum is unconstitutionally burdensome. Now what? The remaining cases, from 1987 through 2014, fall within four categories: stream of commerce, "effects" jurisdiction, jurisdiction based on presence, and general jurisdiction. Let's see what each adds to the *Shoe* analysis.

Stream-of-Commerce

The classic stream-of-commerce scenario is this: D manufactures a component in State X. D sells it to a widget manufacturer in State Y. The widget manufacturer uses D's components in its widgets and sells the widgets to customers in State Z. The component in one of these widgets explodes in State Z, injuring P in State Z. P sues D in State Z. Does D have a relevant contact with State Z?

In *Asahi Metal Industry Co. v. Superior Court*, 480 U.S. 102 (1987), the Court addressed this scenario and failed to provide a definitive rationale. It split into two camps of four justices each. The ninth justice (Stevens) refused to take sides definitively. According to Justice Brennan, there is a relevant contact if D put the product into the stream of commerce and could reasonably anticipate that it would be used in State Z. This theory is consistent with the fact that D makes money because there is a market in State Z. Because there is a market for the widgets (which use D's component) in State Z, D sells more of its components. Thus, D is making money from State Z, which constitutes purposeful availment.

According to Justice O'Connor, there is no contact unless—in addition to what Justice Brennan required—D had an intent to serve the market in State Z. D must have targeted State Z in some way—perhaps by advertising there, or by providing customer service there. Without this additional targeting of State Z, D's component got into State Z only through the unilateral act of a third party, which, under *World-Wide*, cannot constitute purposeful availment.

Which theory—Brennan or O'Connor—is right? Both and neither. Each got four votes, so neither is "the law."[8] This unfortunate state of affairs was compounded 24 years later in *J. J. McIntyre Machinery Ltd. v. Nicastro*, 131 S.Ct. 2780 (2011). There, a British corporation sold its finished products to a separate company in Ohio. The Ohio company then sold the machines (which were large metal-cutting devices for use in scrap metal operations) to businesses in various states. P was injured in New Jersey while using the machine his employer had bought from the Ohio company. Because the Ohio company was bankrupt, P sued the British corporation in New Jersey.

---

[8]   Though the justices disagreed on whether there was a relevant contact between the defendant and the forum, all nine agreed that jurisdiction would not be fair. This is the only case in which the Court has rejected jurisdiction based upon considerations of fairness (the others concluded that the defendant lacked a relevant contact with the forum). But the facts were extraordinary. By the time it got to the Supreme Court, the dispute was between a Taiwanese corporation and a Japanese corporation and the claim was not related to the forum (California). There was no reason to have any American court proceed with the matter.

In _McIntyre_, the Court held, 6-to-3, that New Jersey lacked jurisdiction. There is no binding rationale, however, because the six justices rejecting jurisdiction adopted different views of the situation. Four justices (led by Justice Kennedy) essentially adopted the O'Connor view from _Asahi_. Though the British corporation wanted the Ohio company to sell as many machines as possible, it did not specifically target New Jersey. This opinion says that D must "submit" to jurisdiction in a given state, which might require a greater degree of purposeful availment than we have seen before. Because only four justices signed it, though, this is not "the law." Two other justices refused to choose between the O'Connor and the Brennan view from _Asahi_, and concluded that neither one was met on the facts. Because apparently only one machine had been sold into New Jersey, they reasoned, there was no "stream" of commerce into the state.

The three dissenters essentially adopted the Brennan view from _Asahi_ and concluded that the British corporation, in selling to the Ohio company, could anticipate that its machines would get to New Jersey and that it would be sued there. The British company had targeted the entire United States, and the three dissenters concluded that it would have a relevant contact with any state into which its machines were sold and injured someone.

So the uncertainty sown by _Asahi_ continues. This is a bad thing for real-world lawyers trying to determine when their clients will be subject to personal jurisdiction. It is a great thing, though, for law professors because we can ask you a stream-of-commerce question and expect you to discuss both the O'Connor and the Brennan approach (as well as any other approach your professor may posit).

"Effects" Jurisdiction

It has long been clear that a defendant can have a relevant contact under *Shoe* without entering the forum state. In *Calder v. Jones,* 465 U.S. 783 (1984), the Court upheld jurisdiction in California over the writer and the editor of a National Enquirer story that defamed P. Defamation is an intentional tort, and consists of the publication of a falsehood about P that harms P's reputation. The defendants wrote and edited the story in Florida. The story alleged that P, an actress who lived in California, was drunk on the set of a movie. The Court noted that the defendants relied on phone calls to California sources, wrote the story about activities in California, and caused reputational harm there. The defendants intentionally caused an effect in the forum because California was the focus of the story and of the harm to P.

Thirty years later, the Court considered "effects" jurisdiction in *Walden v. Fiore,* 134 S.Ct. 1115 (2014). There, a police officer working for federal security at the Atlanta airport (D) seized cash belonging to the plaintiffs, who resided in Las Vegas. D prepared an allegedly false affidavit, which he forwarded to law enforcement, saying that the money was connected to illegal drug activity (which would justify its seizure). It turned out the money was from legal gambling and had nothing to do with drugs. The government returned the money, after which the plaintiffs sued D for violating their constitutional rights. They sued in Nevada and argued that jurisdiction was proper because the brunt of D's action was suffered there. Unanimously, the Court rejected jurisdiction. *Calder* requires that D form a contact with the forum. It is not met simply because *the plaintiff* has a relationship (such as residence) with the forum. The plaintiffs lacked access to their money in Nevada not because D did anything there, but because that is where they chose to live.

Jurisdiction Based on Presence

The classic "traditional basis" for *in personam* jurisdiction under *Pennoyer* was service of process on D in the forum. It has long been clear that service within the forum is not *required* to establish jurisdiction. Does that mean, though, that service of process on D in the forum is not adequate to *establish in personam* jurisdiction?

The Court faced the question in *Burnham v. Superior Court*, 495 U.S. 604 (1990). A woman living in California sued her ex-husband for child support in California. The ex-husband was a citizen of New Jersey and the claim arose in New Jersey. The ex-husband was served with process while in California for a few days on business and to visit his children, who lived there with his ex-wife. Because the claim arose outside the forum, the case involved general *in personam* jurisdiction. The question was perfectly cast: does service of process on D in the forum give the court general *in personam* jurisdiction? Unfortunately, as in *Asahi*, the justices split four-to-four (with Justice Stevens again refusing to take sides definitively). So we have no definitive law on the question.

Four justices (led by Justice Scalia) concluded that the traditional basis of *Pennoyer* continues to have independent significance. *Shoe* is irrelevant because *Shoe* did not overrule the traditional bases. This reading has support in *Shoe* itself— remember that the Court there said that its new test would apply *if the defendant were not present in the forum when served with process*. And because D's voluntary presence in the forum when served has always given general *in personam* jurisdiction, the fact that the claim did not arise in the forum was not a problem.

Four other justices (led by Justice Brennan) concluded that the traditional bases were swept away by *Shoe*. Every case must be assessed under *Shoe*. These justices relied on the intervening *quasi-in-rem* case of *Shaffer v. Heitner*, 433 U.S. 186 (1977) (which is discussed in § D). *Shaffer* had broad language saying that *Shoe* was to govern in every case. In context, *Shaffer* may have been saying that *Shoe* was to govern *in rem* and *quasi-in-rem cases*, and not that it had replaced the traditional bases of *in personam* jurisdiction. Whatever one thinks of the argument, the Brennan opinion gets goofy when it tries to justify general jurisdiction over D. In a moment, we will see that general jurisdiction is exercised only if D has significant ties with the forum. In *Burnham*, D had visited California for less than a week, yet Justice Brennan concluded that he had soaked up enough benefits from the state to make him amenable to general jurisdiction.

General and Specific Jurisdiction

As noted above, *in personam* jurisdiction is either specific or general. With specific, the claim against D arises from something D did (or an effect she caused) in the forum. With general, D can be sued in the forum for a claim that arose anywhere in the world. The Court has only addressed general jurisdiction directly in four cases. In the first two, *Perkins v. Benguet Consolidated Mining Co.*, 342 U.S. 437 (1952) and *Helicopteros Nacionales de Colombia, S.A. v. Hall*, 466 U.S. 408 (1984), the Court adopted language from *Shoe* to the effect that general jurisdiction is proper if D has "continuous and systematic" or "substantial" connections with the forum.

More recently, the Court has limited the concept. In *Goodyear Dunlop Tires Operations, S.A. v. Brown*, 131 S.Ct. 2846 (2011), the Court rejected general jurisdiction over European tire manufacturers sued in North Carolina regarding a van wreck in France. The Court said two noteworthy things. First, general jurisdiction cannot be based upon a stream-of-commerce theory.

Some of the defendants' tires had found their way into North Carolina through the stream of commerce, but general jurisdiction cannot be based merely on buying or selling in the forum. The implication is that the defendant must have some physical presence in the forum.

Second, and more importantly, for general jurisdiction, the defendant must not only have continuous and systematic ties with the forum—it must be "at home" there. For a human, the paradigm is the state of her domicile; she is at home there and can be sued there on a claim that arose anywhere. For a corporation, the Court said, paradigms are the state where it is incorporated (formed) and the state in which it has its principal place of business.

> Example: L.L. Bean sells millions of dollars of merchandise in California, though it is incorporated and has its principal place of business on the east coast. Its level of activity in California may be "substantial and continuous," but will not support general jurisdiction because it consists only of purchases and sales.

> Example: Wal-Mart has regional centers and dozens of stores in California, in which it employs thousands of workers. Before *Goodyear*, many people thought that Wal-Mart would be subject to general jurisdiction in California because it had such substantial and continuous ties with that state, not to mention physical presence through stores and administrative offices. After *Goodyear*, however, it seem clear that California cannot exercise general jurisdiction over Wal-Mart. Wal-Mart is not incorporated in California, nor is its principal place of business there.

In *Daimler AG v. Bauman*, 134 S.Ct. 746 (2014), the Court emphatically restated what it said in *Goodyear*. Though it left open the theoretical possibility that a corporate defendant might be "at home" other than where incorporated and where it has its principal place of business, such cases will be few and far between. Almost always, general jurisdiction will be proper only in the two paradigmatic places.

Buried in a footnote in *Daimler* is a surprising statement: when D is at home in the forum, general jurisdiction will be upheld without consideration of reasonableness or of the "fairness factors" noted above. In other words, the two-part analysis from *World-Wide* and *Burger King*, in which the finding of a relevant contact will lead to assessment of whether jurisdiction is fair, does not apply in general jurisdiction cases.

What About the Internet?

The Court decided no personal jurisdiction cases between 1990 and 2011. It decided four cases between 2011 and 2014. None involved jurisdiction based upon Internet activity. If D sends an e-mail to P in another state intended to cause P to suffer emotional distress, there is no reason not to apply *Calder* and uphold jurisdiction. Tougher cases involve claims arising from the operation of a blog. State and lower federal courts are attempting to adapt *Shoe* to such technology.

C. Statutory Provisions for *In Personam* Jurisdiction

The fact that jurisdiction would be constitutional does not mean that the court has jurisdiction. Personal jurisdiction is not automatically conferred on courts. It must be given, which is the job of the legislature. So there must be a statute that permits the court to exercise personal jurisdiction.

Example: D is a lifelong citizen and resident of State X. He is sued in State X and D is properly served with process in State X. There is no question that the exercise of *in personam* jurisdiction over D in State X would be constitutional. But the courts of State X (and the federal courts in State X) do not have jurisdiction, however, unless State X has a statute the permits jurisdiction.

In every state, there will be a statutory basis for *in personam* jurisdiction over a defendant who is domiciled (usually the statute says "resides") in the state or who is served with process in the state. These statutes usually provide for general jurisdiction. In addition, each state has a nonresident motorist statute, which will be similar to that upheld in *Hess v. Pawloski*. By definition, these statutes apply only when D is a nonresident of the forum. (If she were a resident, we would be able to use the statute giving general jurisdiction over those who reside in the forum.) These are specific jurisdiction statutes, and grant jurisdiction over D only for claims arising in the forum—in this case, claims arising from D's operation of a motor vehicle in the forum.

And every state has a "long-arm statute." These were passed in the wake of *Shoe* and expanded jurisdiction beyond nonresident motorist statutes.[9] These statutes apply only to nonresidents of the forum. They vary from state to state, but generally fall within one of two types: the "California" type or the "laundry list" type. The California-type statute is one sentence long, and provides that the courts of that state have jurisdiction to the full extent allowed

---

[9] It would make sense for state legislatures to combine their nonresident motorist statutes with their long-arm statutes into one provision dealing with jurisdiction over non-residents. Generally, they have not done so, apparently because the two were passed at different times. Motorist statutes generally were passed in the 1920s and 1930s and, as we saw in *Hess*, were based upon implied consent. Long-arms were passed in the 1940s and 1950s and were based upon the contacts and fairness rationale of *International Shoe*.

by the Constitution. In these states, then, the statutory analysis for personal jurisdiction is the same as the constitutional test.

The laundry list type of statute is more detailed. It lists various things a nonresident defendant can do to subject herself to *in personam* jurisdiction in the forum. These are usually specific jurisdiction statutes, so the nonresident is being sued for something she did (or an effect she caused) in the forum. These statutes vary considerably, but classic examples are that D (1) committed a tortious act in the forum or (2) contracted to supply goods or services in the forum or (3) transacted business in the forum, or (4) owns or uses real property (land) in the forum. If P has a claim against a nonresident, and the claim arises from the nonresident's doing any of these things in the forum, the statute grants jurisdiction.

Study the long-arm language closely. There is a big difference between requiring that D "transacted *any* business" and that D "transacted *substantial* business" in the forum. Likewise, there could be a big difference between requiring that D committed a "tort" in the forum or requiring that she committed a "tortious act or omission" in the forum. Beyond that, note that courts may interpret identical language differently. A good example concerns statutes that allow jurisdiction over one who commits a tortious act or omission in the forum.

> Example: D manufactures widgets in State A and markets the widgets in State A and in State B. P, who resides in State B, orders a widget from D. D ships the widget to P in State B. The widget malfunctions and injures P in State B. The State B long-arm statute provides for jurisdiction over a non-resident (D is a non-resident of State B) who "commits a tortious act or omission in State B." P alleges that D committed a tortious act or

omission (by manufacturing a faulty widget, which injured P). But did D commit any such tort in State B?

Some courts say no, because, to the extent that D was negligent, she was negligent in State A (where she made the widget). These courts emphasize the words "act or omission" and conclude that D simply did not do (or omit to do) anything in State B. This position was adopted by the New York Court of Appeals in *Feathers v. McLucas*, 209 N.E.2d 68 (N.Y. 1968). On the other hand, some courts say yes, on the theory that the negligent manufacture of the widget did not become tortious until P was injured. And because P was injured in State B, D committed a tortious act or omission in State B. These courts emphasize the word "tortious" and conclude that there is no tort until there is an injury. This position was adopted by the Illinois Supreme Court in *Gray v. American Radiator & Standard Sanitary Corp.*, 176 N.E.2d 761 (Ill. 1961).

Which position—*Feathers* or *Gray*—is correct? Both are defensible interpretations of the statutory language and herein lies a secret of law school success: if your professor covered this (or any other) split of authority, be prepared to discuss both approaches on the exam.

By the way, after the New York Court of Appeals interpreted that statutory language in a restrictive way, the New York legislature amended the long-arm. It kept the language we saw above, which had been interpreted not to apply to the example we just saw. And it added a new provision to cover cases in which the tortious act or omission occurred *outside the forum* but the tortious injury occurred *in the forum*. The statute then requires additional contacts by D with the forum. Several states have adopted this language, so you may study a provision that permits specific jurisdiction when D commits a tort *out of state* that injures P *in the forum*, provided that D also has some other substantial tie with the forum—typically, that D derives substantial revenue from interstate commerce or from sales in the forum.

Two points before we finish this section. First, be ready to apply a statute (probably a long-arm statute) on the exam. Pay especial attention to any statutes your professor discussed in class. Second, even though these statutes are passed by state legislatures and thus apply in state courts, the federal courts apply them as well. Under FRCP 4(k)(1)(A), in the ordinary civil case, federal courts can exercise personal jurisdiction only if a state court in the state in which they sit could exercise personal jurisdiction. So even though the case may be in federal court in Virginia, the Virginia statutes on personal jurisdiction will apply.

D.   *In Rem* and *Quasi-in-Rem* Jurisdiction

As we have seen, a valid *in personam* judgment creates a personal obligation for D to pay P. P will always want to get an *in personam* judgment if she can, for precisely that reason. But sometimes P cannot get *in personam* jurisdiction. For example, maybe jurisdiction would be constitutional but the forum's long-arm statute is interpreted narrowly and does not apply. When P cannot sue *in personam*, but D has property in the forum, P will try the next best thing: suing *in rem* or *quasi-in-rem (QIR)*. With *in rem* and *QIR*, jurisdiction is exercised not over D herself, but over her property.

The property over which the court exercises *in rem* or *QIR* jurisdiction must be present in the forum state. It might be real property (land) or other tangible property (like a wristwatch or a car). It might be intangible property (such as a brokerage account or a copyright). The property is called the "res."

What's the difference between *in rem* and *QIR*? Here we need a bit of detail (that some professors do not get into). Technically, there are two types of QIR: type 1 (*QIR-1*) and type 2 (*QIR-2*). With *QIR-1* and *in rem* cases, the litigation is about who owns that property at issue. So in *in rem* and *QIR-1*, we use property as the jurisdictional predicate and the point of the litigation is to determine who owns that property.[10]

With *QIR-2*, the litigation has nothing to do with who owns the res. Everybody knows it belongs to D. The claim against D is for anything *other than the ownership of the res*. A great example comes from *Mitchell v. Neff*, which was the case that underlay *Pennoyer*. Mitchell was a lawyer. He alleged that Neff retained him and then did not pay. It was a simple breach of contract case, for about $300. Mitchell sued Neff in Oregon. Neff had moved to California in the meantime, so was not present in Oregon. Mitchell could not get *in personam* jurisdiction over Neff because he could not have Neff served with process in Oregon (remember, this is in the nineteenth century, long before *Shoe*). But Neff owned land in Oregon. So Mitchell tried to use Neff's land as the jurisdictional predicate. It was a *QIR-2* case because (1) Neff's land was the res on which jurisdiction was based and (2) the claim against Neff had nothing to do with who owned the property.

It would have worked, too, except for one thing. The court in which Mitchell sued failed to attach the res *at the outset of the case*. It did attach the case after Neff had failed to respond to the suit, but that was too late.[11] Jurisdiction depends upon power over

---

[10] So what's the difference between *in rem* and *QIR-1*? A judgment *QIR-1* binds only the parties to the litigation, so either P or D ends up owning the property. Technically, a judgment *in rem* binds not just these parties but the entire world on the question of who owns the res. How can a judgment bind the whole world? The answer is rooted in history that is beyond our scope. Suffice to say that true *in rem* cases are rare. An example is a proceeding in admiralty to determine the ownership of a vessel. By customary law, the court with jurisdiction over the vessel can determine who owns it and, in theory, that judgment binds everyone.

[11] The property was not attached until after default judgment was entered against Neff. The purpose of attaching property at that point is to have it sold to satisfy the judgment. We talked about that in the last two paragraphs of Chapter 1. What we deal with here is totally different. Here we talk about using property as the

the jurisdictional predicate at the beginning of the suit. Otherwise, the property could be sold or given away before judgment was entered, and the entire court proceeding would be a waste of time. Because the property was not seized at the outset of the case, the *QIR-2* judgment was void.

Under *Pennoyer*, then, a judgment *in rem* or *QIR* would be valid if the res on which jurisdiction is based is seized by the court at the outset of the case. (Remember, as in any case, D must be given notice, as we'll see in § F.) That was the law for 99 years, until *Shaffer v. Heitner* (1977). There, the Court addressed the impact of *Shoe* on *in rem* and *QIR* jurisdiction. It recognized that a judgment *in rem* or *QIR* is simply an indirect way to affect D. Thus, under *Shaffer*, *in rem* and *QIR* are proper only if D's contacts with the forum satisfy *Shoe*. D herself—not simply her property—must have such contacts with the forum that the exercise of jurisdiction does not offend traditional notions of fair play and substantial justice. In other words, the constitutional test for *in rem* and *QIR* is the same as the constitutional test for *in personam* jurisdiction.[12]

Due process continues to require that the res be attached at the outset of the suit. So even D's contacts with the forum satisfy *International Shoe*, the court must seize the res when the case begins.

In rem or *QIR* jurisdiction is not automatically conferred on a jurisdiction's courts. There must be a statute that allows the court to seize the res and exercise *in rem* and *QIR* jurisdiction. We are not talking here about long-arm statutes. Those are for *in personam* jurisdiction. Here, we are talking about "attachment

---

jurisdictional predicate for suit itself, and not as a source of funds once a valid judgment is entered.

[12] The fact that D owns the property is itself a contact between D and the forum for *Shoe* purposes.

statutes." Every state has one, and they do not vary much from state to state. They usually provide that the jurisdiction may attach property within the state that D "owns or claims to own." This is great language—"owns" covers *QIR-2* and "claims to own" covers *in rem* and *QIR-1*. The statutes require (as does due process) that the attachment take place at the outset of the case. P usually will file the complaint and then arrange immediately for the attachment.[13] Again, though these are state statutes, they generally apply (just as state statutes for *in personam* apply) in federal court as well.

E.   Approach for the Exam

Unless your professor tells you to write a history essay, do not do so. Your job is to *apply present doctrine* to the facts on the exam and reach a reasonable conclusion. Your professor may suggest an analytical approach to an essay question regarding personal jurisdiction. If so, follow that. If she does not, however, you might consider this approach.

1. Statute

The first step is to determine whether a statute permits personal jurisdiction on the facts of the case. If there is no applicable statute, there is no personal jurisdiction—even if personal jurisdiction would be constitutional. And remember that any arguably applicable statute will be a state statute. This is true even in federal court; we look to state statutes for personal jurisdiction.

---

[13] The attachment may be physical in the sense that the court directs an appropriate officer (maybe the sheriff) to take custody of the res. With real property, the court will direct that signs be posted on the land indicating the seizure and will also have appropriate notice placed in the land records, so the defendant will not be able to sell it or give it away in the meantime.

If it's an *in personam* case, the statute might be based upon one of the traditional bases, such granting jurisdiction over one domiciled in the forum state or over a defendant who was served with process in the state. More likely, though, the defendant will be a nonresident who is not served with process in the forum. Every state has two statutes to deal with such defendants: a nonresident motorist statute and a long-arm statute. These statutes tend to grant specific in personam jurisdiction, which means that the claim asserted against D must arise from something D did (or an effect D caused) in the forum.

Study the statutory language very carefully. It might say that D must have transacted "substantial" business in the forum. This is quite different from merely requiring that D transact "any" business in the forum. (Whatever you studied in class in this regard may be a tip-off of what to expect.) Remember too that the same language may be interpreted differently, as shown about the disagreement about whether a "tort" occurs where P is injured or where D did whatever she did (see the second Example in § C).

If the case is *in rem* or *QIR*, the statute will be an attachment statute (see § D). It will require that the court attach property that D "owns or claims to own." The property must be in the forum and the court must attach it at the outset of the case.

If a statute is met—or arguably met—then we go to the second step of the analysis, which is to assess whether exercise of jurisdiction would be constitutional.

2. Constitution

If it is an *in personam* case, it is a good idea to identify whether the facts fit one of the traditional bases from *Pennoyer*. This is important because of *Burnham*. In that case, the Court split four-to-four on whether traditional bases are an alternative to *Shoe* or whether they were replaced by *Shoe* (§ B). If one applies, tell your professor that four justices in *Burnham* would find that fact sufficient, without the need to assess *Shoe*. But, because four justices held that *Shoe* always applies, you need to go on and apply *Shoe*. And, of course, you will apply *Shoe* to any case in which a traditional basis does not apply.

Now, how do we apply *Shoe*? Your professor might have taken a position on whether cases like *J. McIntyre* have changed the approach prescribed in *World-Wide* and *Burger King*. Most seem to think they have not. So, we apply *Shoe* as explicated there. Though those cases spoke of a two-step approach (contact followed by fairness/reasonableness), in fact there is an implicit third focus of analysis: whether the claim arises from D's contact with the forum.

First, there must be a relevant *contact* between D and the forum. A relevant contact is one that results from purposeful availment by D, and not from the unilateral act of a third party. In addition, *World-Wide* says that a relevant contact is one that renders it foreseeable that D would get sued in this forum. Your job here will be to analogize—are the facts more like *McGee* (in which D solicited business from the forum) or like *Hanson* and *World-Wide* (in which the contact with the forum was the act of a third party)? There is no right answer here, so argue both ways and come to a reasonable conclusion. Your conclusion is not as important as your analysis.

Second, if there is a relevant contact (or arguably so), then ask one question: does P's claim arise from D's contact with the forum? If the answer is yes, we have an example of "specific" *in personam* jurisdiction. If the answer is no, we can have jurisdiction only if we meet the test for "general" jurisdiction. Under *Goodyear* and *Daimler AG*, this requires that D have such continuous and systematic ties with the forum that she be considered "essentially at home" there. For a human, this includes her state of domicile. For a corporation, it includes the state in which incorporated and the state in which the company has its principal place of business.

Third, assess whether jurisdiction would be *fair or reasonable* under the circumstances. (*Daimler AG* says this step does not apply in general jurisdiction cases.) On the exam, you are likely to get specific jurisdiction so you may expressly address this. In *Burger King* and other cases, the Court has listed five factors relevant to the inquiry: (1) inconvenience for D and her witnesses (in having to travel to the forum), (2) forum state's interest, (3) P's interest in litigating in the forum, (4) the legal system's interest in efficiency, and (5) shared substantive policies of the states.

D bears a heavy burden here. She must show that the forum is so "gravely" inconvenient that she is at a severe disadvantage. Remember, your grade does not depend on being able to list the factors. It depends on recognizing facts that are relevant to the factors. Assume that every fact is on the exam for a reason. Suppose the exam said that P was badly injured. This might be inviting you to explain that this relates to factor (3)—P could not easily travel to D's home state for suit. Suppose the exam says that P, who was injured, is a police officer. Maybe this is relevant to factor (2)—the state has an interest in having public servants obtain justice. Be aggressive!

Finally, if the case is *in rem* or *QIR*, and the attachment statute is satisfied and the res is attached at the outset of the case, explain whether it is *in rem*, *QIR-1*, or *QIR-2*. Tell the professor that *Shaffer* requires that D's contacts with the forum satisfy *Shoe*. Undertake the *Shoe* analysis.

In personal jurisdiction, the "answer" is usually not clear. So don't worry about it. Walk your professor through an analytical approach and come to a reasonable conclusion. Use the facts—

make it fun. You will know the law—go on a scavenger hunt for relevant facts.

F. Notice and Opportunity to Be Heard

In addition to personal jurisdiction, due process requires that anyone bound by a court order must have had her "day in court." This means that she must be given a realistic opportunity to appear and present her side of the story. We will see in Chapter 8 that some non-parties (that is, persons never formally joined as litigants in a case) may be bound by a judgment. This can be done, however, only if their interests are adequately represented by a litigant. In these narrow situations, the "day in court" is provided by representation. (We discuss this in Chapter 9, § C.)

We are not concerned with those cases here. Instead, we address the classic manner in which one is accorded her day in court: she is joined as a party and brought before the jurisdiction of the court. A plaintiff automatically has party status and is before the jurisdiction of the court, simply by filing suit. A defendant is named as such in the complaint. Beyond that, however, due process requires that she be given notice of the suit and an opportunity to be heard. In nearly every case, this is done by "service" of "process." Each state has its own rules for service of process. We focus on Federal Rule 4, which governs in federal court.[14]

"Process" consists of two documents: (1) the summons and (2) a copy of the complaint. The summons is issued by the court, and informs D that she has been sued, she must respond within 21 days (or risk default), and gives other information about the court and the case (see FRCP 4(a)(1)). The complaint is the document filed by P, which informs D of P's claims against her. Together,

---

[14] The Supreme Court promulgates the FRCP. Congress delegated this task to the Court in the Rules Enabling Act, which we discuss in Chapter 10, § C.

then, these documents give D notice of the proceeding and why she has been sued and tell her how, when, and where to respond to proceed through the litigation process.

"Service" refers to the method by which the process is given to D. For generations, law enforcement officers, such as United States Marshals, performed the function. Today, however, in federal court, any non-party who is at least 18 years old may serve process; no court order is required (see FRCP 4(c)(2)). (Some state provisions require that the court appoint a civilian process-server.)

In *Mullane v. Central Hanover Bank & Trust Co.*, 339 U.S. 306 (1950), the Supreme Court established the due process requirement for notice: it must be "reasonably calculated, under all the circumstances, to apprise interested parties of the pendency of the action and afford them an opportunity to present their objections." Service of process in compliance with the provisions of Rule 4 will be constitutional. What gets iffy are cases in which P provides only notice by publication. This was routine for *in rem* and *QIR* cases in earlier eras. After *Mullane*, however, in any kind of case—*in personam*, *in rem*, or *QIR*—service by publication is an absolute last resort. If the name and an address of the persons to be affected by a proceeding is known, publication notice cannot be "reasonably calculated" to afford actual notice. Some other method must be tried.

Service on a Human Defendant (A "Natural Person")

Rule 4(e) governs service of process on human defendants. Start with Rule 4(e)(2), which provides three alternative methods. One, "personal service" (FRCP 4(e)(2)(A)) is exactly what it sounds like: the process server hands the documents to D. This can be done anywhere in the forum state, and need not be perfected at D's home or office. On YouTube, you can see Ciara being served with process while singing at a concert.

Two, the requirements for "substituted service" (FRCP 4(e)(2)(B)) are very strict: (1) this must be accomplished at D's dwelling or usual abode, (2) service must be left with one of "suitable age and discretion," and (3) the person with whom it is left must reside there. There are many possibilities here for the exam. We might have a wealthy defendant with ten homes around the world, raising a question of whether the place where service was attempted was his dwelling or usual abode. Courts usually uphold service if D was living there at the time. Then we could have service on a 16-year-old honors student. Is that someone of suitable age and discretion? Then we could add that the person on whom service was made was staying at D's house for six weeks in the summer. Does that person reside at the home? The answers to these questions are less important that being able to argue—one the one hand yes, on the other hand no. Come to a reasonable conclusion, but do not make the mistake of thinking that your grade will be based on whether you get the "right" answer. There is no "right" answer. There are good arguments and reasonable answers.

The third possibility for serving process on a human is to serve her agent. Many of the things we can do in this life can be delegated. The person we authorize to act on our behalf is our agent. If we authorize someone to receive service of process on our behalf, service on the agent is effective. Sometimes this is done by contract. Sometimes this is done by operation of law, as with nonresident motorist statutes, discussed in § C.

In addition to the foregoing, Rule 4(e)(1) permits use of any method for serving process that is allowed by *state law*—either of the state in which the federal court sits or in which service is effective. The Federal Rules have no general provision allowing service of process by mail. State statutes routinely do, at least in some kinds of cases. Those state provisions can be used in federal civil cases.

Service on a Business

Rule 4(h)(1)(B) allows service on any form of business to be made by serving an officer, managing or general agent, or other agent authorized by law to receive process. Suppose service is made on the person overseeing operation of the company's assembly line. Is that person a "managing or general agent?" It depends on the realities rather than title. So if she has such responsibilities that one would expect her to communicate important messages, service will probably be upheld. In addition, do not overlook Rule 4(h)(1)(A), which permits use of methods of service permitted by *state law*, just as we saw above with regard to humans.

Waiver of Service by Mail

Rule 4(d) permits the parties to use mail to *waive* the need for formal service of process. P mails to D a form notifying D of the suit, a copy of the complaint, two copies of a waiver form, and a self-addressed stamped envelope. D then has 30 days after mailing of these materials in which to sign a waiver form and mail it back to P (in the envelope provided). P then files the waiver form in court, at which point the waiver of the need for formal service is effective. Importantly, by waiving service, D does not waive the right to object to personal jurisdiction or venue. Also, she has 60 days from P's mailing the material in which to respond to the complaint (this is longer than she gets if she's served with process). If D fails to return the waiver form in a timely fashion, P will have service effected. Unless D has an excuse for not returning the waiver form, D will be required to pay the costs of that service.

Geographic Limit

Rule 4(k)(1)(A) provides that process can be served anywhere within the state in which the federal court sits. So if the case is filed in federal court in San Diego, process may be served on D anywhere in California, even 840 miles away near the Oregon border. On the other hand, service can be made outside the state in which the federal court sits only if *state law* allows. This is consistent with the notion we saw in § C that federal courts can exercise personal jurisdiction outside the state in which they sit only if the state court could. It is likely that federal courts could be empowered to exercise nationwide personal jurisdiction power, based upon a defendant's contacts anywhere in the United States. But, as a matter of comity, Rule 4 provides that the federal courts limit their personal jurisdiction power to that of the state in which they sit.

BTW, this section has been about formal service of process (or waiver thereof), which is necessary to bring D before the jurisdiction of the court. After this is accomplished, the parties "serve" other documents (like answers, motions, discovery) on each other. No summons is required for those. Those documents can be served under Rule 5(b)(2) by delivery, mail, or (if the party agrees) e-mail.

Selecting a Forum: Subject Matter Jurisdiction

A. Overview

Personal jurisdiction tells the plaintiff (P) that she may sue the defendant (D) in a particular state (or states). Now we turn to a different question: in which court (in that state) will P sue? Specifically, will she sue in a federal trial court (federal district court) or will she sue in the state trial court (the name of which varies from state to state)? This is the question of subject matter jurisdiction. Remember: personal jurisdiction is exercised over *parties*. Subject matter jurisdiction is exercised over *cases*. To enter a valid judgment, the court must have both personal jurisdiction and subject matter jurisdiction.

State courts have "general" subject matter jurisdiction, which means they can hear any cognizable claim.[1]

---

[1]   There are a few narrow exceptions to this. As we will see in the last paragraph of § C, a few federal question cases can *only* be brought in federal court. Most federal claims, however, can be heard in state or federal court.

Example: P, a citizen of Australia, wants to sue D, a citizen of Bolivia, concerning a car wreck between the two, which occurred in South Africa. May a state court in North Dakota hear this case? Yes. State courts can hear any kind of case. (There may be a personal jurisdiction issue, because D may not have sufficient contacts with South Dakota to justify personal jurisdiction, but that is a separate question.)

Federal courts, in contrast, have "limited" subject matter jurisdiction. They can only hear certain types of cases. The federal government is one of limited powers. Article III of the Constitution sets the outer boundary of cases that can be heard in federal courts. Generally, the subject matter jurisdiction of Article III is not self-executing. Congress must pass a statute granting subject matter jurisdiction to the federal courts. The two major grants of federal subject matter jurisdiction are (1) diversity of citizenship and (2) federal question cases.

The fact that a case satisfies one of those grants of federal jurisdiction does not require the parties to litigate in federal court. Remember, state courts generally can hear any kind of case, so P may choose to file her case in state court. In most instances when a case will invoke federal subject matter jurisdiction, there will be "concurrent" subject matter jurisdiction—meaning that the case could be heard either in federal or state court. We will see below, however, that D might be able to "remove" the case from state to federal court. But let's start by getting a case into federal court as an initial matter.

B. Diversity of Citizenship Jurisdiction

Article III permits federal courts to hear cases "between citizens of different states." These cases go to federal court not because some federal law applies—indeed, these cases are governed by state law, as seen in Chapter 10. Instead, they go to federal court because the litigants are "citizens of different states." The historic justification of diversity jurisdiction is that it provides a federal forum for disputes in which one litigant might fear local bias in the state courts. Why does the type of court matter? As we saw in Chapter 1, § B, many state judges are elected, which means a non-local litigant might worry that the judge, to maintain good relations with the electorate, might rule in favor of a local litigant. And state juries are drawn from a small geographic area. In federal court, these worries are allayed. Federal judges serve lifetime terms, their pay cannot be reduced, and they never face an electorate. This political insulation ensures that they can rule without fear of voter reprisal. Moreover, juries in federal courts are drawn from the entire district, which always consists of multiple counties. So a federal jury may be less parochial.

Congress has granted diversity jurisdiction to the federal courts in 28 U.S.C. § 1332(a)(1).[2] It establishes two requirements. First, the case must be between "citizens of different States." Second, the amount in controversy must exceed $75,000.

First Requirement: Citizens of Different States (The Complete Diversity Rule)

The starting point for all diversity cases is the complete diversity rule, which Chief Justice John Marshall established for the Supreme Court in *Strawbridge v. Curtiss*, 7 U.S. 267 (1806). That case holds that the statute granting diversity of citizenship jurisdiction requires that every plaintiff be of different citizenship from every defendant. (The statute has never actually said that, but because Congress has never done anything to change the result

---

[2]   This is a statute passed by Congress, in Title 28 of the United States Code. It is not a Federal Rule of Civil Procedure. Those are promulgated by the Supreme Court.

of *Strawbridge*, it is treated as a statutory requirement.) So there is no jurisdiction under § 1332(a)(1) if *any* plaintiff is a citizen of the same state as *any* defendant.

> Example: P, a citizen of California, sues 1000 defendants, 999 of whom are Arizona citizens and one of whom is a California citizen. The case fails to invoke diversity jurisdiction because it violates the complete diversity rule.

You are entering a profession in which words matter. Every year, professors seem to see at least one exam in which a student discusses the complete diversity rule by saying: "all litigants must be of diverse citizenship." That is wrong. Plaintiffs can be co-citizens with each other. Defendants can be co-citizens with each other. All plaintiffs must be of diverse citizenship from all defendants.

Speaking of important words: we are concerned here about the *citizenship* of the litigants—not their residence, and not where they are "from." If you filed a complaint in federal court and alleged that P is a "resident" of California or that D is "from" Arizona, the case should be dismissed. Jurisdiction requires allegations of *citizenship*, and that is the term we should use. Be precise.

Citizenship of a Natural Person

A "natural person" is a human (as distinguished from an "artificial person" like a corporation). Any human will do. She does not have to eat tofu to be a "natural" person. Joan Rivers is a natural person. A natural person who is a citizen of the United States is a citizen of the U.S. state in which she is *domiciled*. Domicile is an important concept. For starters, a person has only one domicile at a time. It is impossible to have more than one domicile (so it is impossible for a human to have more than one state of citizenship). Moreover, everybody always has one domicile; there is no such thing as a human without a domicile. Even people who roam the earth aimlessly always have a domicile. Everyone is ascribed a domicile at birth (generally it is the domicile of your mother). When you reach the age of majority, you may change your domicile.

Changing one's domicile requires two things. First, you must be physically present in the new state. Second, you must form the intent to make that state your permanent home. Courts vary somewhat in how they state those requirements, but everyone agrees that there is a physical component and a mental component. Until you meet them both, you retain your previous domicile—even if you have been away from that place for 60 years.

> Example: A New York citizen forms the intent to make Nevada her permanent home. While driving to Nevada, she is involved in a car wreck in Colorado. Her citizenship is still New York because physically she did not get to Nevada.

> Example: A Pennsylvania citizen goes to California for four years of college. Then she goes to law school in Florida for three years, followed by four years of medical school in Hawaii, followed by 40 years as a deckhand on a steamship, sailing around the world. The whole time she is thinking "I never want to go back to Pennsylvania but I just don't know where I want live." She is still a citizen of Pennsylvania, because she has never formed the intent to make another place her permanent home.

Please go back to Chapter 1, § A, to the first indented Example in the book. That will show how the facts relating to domicile might be tested.

Citizenship of a Corporation

A corporation is an entity through which people conduct business. Each state has rules for how to form a corporation. The rules provide that the corporation comes into existence when the appropriate state officer (usually the secretary of state) accepts the required documents for filing. Thus, the founder of the corporation will decide where to form (or "incorporate" or "charter") the business. What is the citizenship of a corporation? Be careful not to use the word "domicile" here. Domicile, as we just saw, is a proxy for the citizenship of a natural person. The citizenship of a corporation is defined by 28 U.S.C. § 1332(c)(1).

That statute defines corporate citizenship as (1) "every State . . . by which it has been incorporated" *and* (2) "the State . . . where it has its principal place of business" (PPB). Words matter. When talking about incorporation, the statute says "every" state, which implies that there could be more than one. But in talking of PPB, the statute says "the" state, which tells us that there is only one. Indeed, theoretically, corporations can be incorporated in more than one state. As a practical matter, this almost never happens anymore, so there will usually be only one state of incorporation. And there is only one place where a corporation has its PPB.

Notice, then, that a corporation (unlike a human) can be a citizen of more than one state at a time. The complete diversity rule applies as it always does.

> Example: Louise, a citizen of Georgia, sues XYZ Corp., which is incorporated in Delaware with its PPB in Pin Point, Georgia. No diversity. On the plaintiff side is a citizen of Georgia. On the defendant's side is a corporation that is a citizen of Delaware *and* Georgia (do not say Delaware *or* Georgia; it is a citizen of *both*

states). Thus, a Georgia citizen is on both sides of the case. Unless there is some other basis of federal subject matter jurisdiction (like federal question jurisdiction), Louise must sue in state court.

Your professor cannot hide the ball on the corporation's state of incorporation. But what about the entity's PPB? After decades of uncertainty, the Supreme Court gave a definitive interpretation in *Hertz Corp. v. Friend,* 559 U.S. 77 (2010). It held that the PPB is the place (remember, there is only one PPB) where the managers "direct, control, and coordinate corporate activities." This is called the "nerve center," and is usually the headquarters.

Citizenship of Unincorporated Businesses

Not all businesses are corporations. There are various other business forms, including the partnership, the limited partnership, and the limited liability company (LLC). Congress has never defined the citizenship of these "unincorporated" businesses. Nonetheless, the courts have been consistent in holding that they are citizens of all states of which their members are citizens. In other words, for these businesses, the state of formation and the state of PPB are irrelevant. Because we look to the citizenship of all members, an unincorporated business might be a citizen of many states. In fact, labor unions usually are unincorporated. So the Teamsters union, with members who are citizens of all 50 states, is deemed a citizen of every state. Accordingly, no case by or against the Teamsters can satisfy the complete diversity rule. The Teamsters thus can never sue or be sued under diversity jurisdiction.[3]

Right now, explain to yourself (not out loud if you're in the library) (1) why a human can only have one state of citizenship, (2)

---

[3]   Is that a problem? No. It can sue or be sued in state court. Or a case involving it might invoke federal question jurisdiction.

why a corporation can have two states of citizenship, and (3) why an unincorporated business can have 50 states of citizenship. One last point. Though § 1332(a)(1) speaks of citizens of a "state," § 1332(e) provides that this includes federal enclaves such as the District of Columbia and Puerto Rico. So even though such places are not "states," they count as such for diversity jurisdiction.

Second Requirement: Amount in Controversy

Congress has always imposed an amount in controversy requirement for diversity of citizenship cases. The reasoning is that the fear of local bias will be greater if the stakes are fairly substantial. Congress increases the amount-in-controversy requirement from time to time to reflect this concern. There is also a sense that federal courts should not be bothered with small-claims matters (at least not in cases, such as these, that involve the application of state (not federal) law).

Even if the citizenship of the parties satisfies the complete diversity rule, the case cannot invoke diversity jurisdiction unless the amount in controversy *exceeds* $75,000. If plaintiff sues for exactly $75,000, the case cannot invoke diversity jurisdiction. The claim must be for at least $75,000.01.[4] Usually, whatever P claims will govern for these purposes unless it is "clear to a legal certainty" that the amount does not exceed $75,000. Such cases are rare. For example, if a statute imposes a cap on recovery for a claim—say, of $50,000—that claim alone cannot invoke diversity jurisdiction.

The most testable aspect of the amount in controversy requirement is "aggregation." Aggregation is when we must add multiple claims to get over $75,000. And the rule is very

---

[4] Quick nerdly professorial aside: Do you see why it drives a professor nuts to read an exam answer that says: "The amount must exceed the statutory requirement of $75,000"? [Answer: The statutory requirement is not $75,000. It is *in excess* of $75,000. So just say "the amount must exceed $75,000."]

straightforward: one P can aggregate all the claims she wants against one D. There is no limit on the number of claims, and the claims may be completely unrelated factually and legally.

> Example: P sues D for (1) $40,000 breach of contract, (2) $50,000 arising from an auto crash between them, and for (3) $60,000 arising from a land transaction between the two. None of the claims alone exceeds $75,000. But because these claims are asserted by one P against one D, we aggregate them, which means we add them. So the amount in controversy in this case is $150,000.

A corollary to this rule is that we cannot aggregate claims between multiple parties. Say P sued two defendants (D-1 and D-2) in one case. The claim against D-1 is for $40,000 and the claim against D-2 is for $50,000. This case cannot invoke diversity jurisdiction. Why? It fails to meet the amount in controversy requirement. Remember, we can only aggregate claims by *one plaintiff against one defendant*. These claims are against two defendants.

There is one nuance to this. If the case involves a joint claim, we look to the value of the claim itself, and the number of parties is irrelevant.

> Example: Three students who bought this book confront the author and say that reading the book was the worst experience of their lives. They then assault the author and pummel him, causing physical injuries of $75,000.01. The author sues the three students. Because this is a joint claim—asserted against joint tortfeasors—we look to the value of the claim. The fact that there are three defendants does not matter. Because this is a joint claim, any of the three can be held liable for the full amount.

So do not go for the head fake about three defendants. Do not treat this as though there were $25,000.01 claims against each of three people and you were trying to aggregate them. Because of joint liability, there are not three claims. There is only one claim, so there is nothing to aggregate. And because the one claim exceeds $75,000, it satisfies the requirement. The same would be true if two plaintiffs, who jointly own land, sued D for trespass and sought damages of $75,000.01. Because they are asserting a joint claim, we look to the value of the claim; the number of parties is irrelevant. The concept of joint (or "undivided" claims) is sometimes difficult to fathom, as you will study in Property. Be on the lookout for the word "joint" (even if you're not in Colorado or Washington). If you see a joint claim, apply this rule.

C. Federal Question Jurisdiction

Article III and 28 U.S.C. § 1331 permit federal courts to hear cases "arising under" federal law. Here, the citizenship of the parties is irrelevant. Federal court access is provided because these cases are governed by federal law. It makes sense that federal judges would develop expertise in such matters and might be sympathetic to the policies underlying federal law. Moreover, there is no amount in controversy requirement in these "federal question" cases. The notion is that the vindication of federal rights should command access to federal courts, even if the harm, as measured in dollars, is not great.

In interpreting the statutory grant of federal question jurisdiction, the Supreme Court has imposed restrictions that are not constitutionally mandated. One is that the federal issue in the case must be "substantial." The case will be dismissed if P's federal claim is frivolous or obviously without merit. A more important restriction for our purposes is the "well-pleaded complaint rule." This requires the court, in determining whether a case "arises under" federal law, to consider only the complaint and to ignore anything filed by the defendant (such as D's answer or counterclaim). Not only that, but in reading the complaint, the court looks only to the claim itself, and ignores extraneous matter P may have pleaded. As a result, it is never enough simply that P's claim mentions or implicates some federal law. Her *claim itself must arise under federal law.*

The famous case is *Louisville & Nashville Railroad Co. v. Mottley,* 211 U.S. 149 (1908). There, Railroad had given the Mottleys a lifetime pass to ride for free (it did so in settlement of a claim by the Mottleys). Congress passed a law (that makes it a federal law, so we should be on the lookout for possible federal question jurisdiction) forbidding railroads from giving away free passes. Because of this law, Railroad refused to honor the Mottleys' pass. The Mottleys sued Railroad. In their complaint, they said (1) Railroad has breached the contract and (2) the new federal law does not apply to us.

So the complaint mentioned federal law. In fact, the only dispute between the parties was over federal law. Railroad agreed that it breached the contract, but asserted that the federal law required it to do so. So the only issue to be decided was federal— whether the new law voided the Mottleys' pass (and, if so, whether it was constitutional). Nonetheless, the case did *not* invoke federal question jurisdiction. The *claim* (part (1), that Railroad breached the contract) was not federal (there is nothing federal about breaching a contract). Part (2) of complaint was not part of the claim. It was the rebuttal of an anticipated defense. Under the well-pleaded complaint rule, it is ignored. We look only at the claim.

There is an easy way to apply the well-pleaded complaint rule: simply ask "is plaintiff enforcing a federal right?" If so, the case arises under federal law. If not, it generally does not.[5] Were the Mottleys enforcing a federal right? No. The federal statute did not give the Mottleys any rights. In fact, it took something away from them. They were trying to *avoid* application of the federal law, so their clearly did not arise under that federal law.

Section 1331 is the "general" federal question statute. There are dozens of specialized grants of federal jurisdiction regarding specific federal claims. A few of the specialized statutes grant *exclusive* federal jurisdiction. For example, claims under the Federal Tort Claims Act, the federal securities and antitrust laws, bankruptcy, as well as patent and copyright infringement cases can only be heard in federal courts. State courts may not hear them. For the overwhelming majority of federal claims, however, there is concurrent subject matter jurisdiction. P can sue in federal or state court.

D. Supplemental Jurisdiction

Supplemental jurisdiction, codified at 28 U.S.C. § 1367, is fundamentally different from diversity of citizenship and federal question jurisdiction. Those two can get a *case* into federal court. Supplemental jurisdiction cannot. Rather, supplemental jurisdiction operates only after the case is already in federal court. Once it is there (because P's claim invoked diversity or federal question jurisdiction), additional claims may be asserted in the case. They might be claims by P or by D or by or against someone brought into the case. It is critical to understand that *every single claim ever asserted in federal court must have federal subject matter jurisdiction.* If they fail to invoke federal

---

[5]   The Court has held that state-created claims can invoke federal question jurisdiction when they raise a substantial federal issue and when allowing federal jurisdiction would not upset the allocation of judicial power between the federal and state governments. *See, e.g., Grable & Sons Metal Prods. v. Darue*, 545 U.S. 308 (2005). Such cases are few and very far between.

subject matter jurisdiction, they cannot be asserted in the pending case and may be pursued only in state court.

So we must assess every claim ever joined in federal court (not just the original claim by P versus D, but every claim) to see whether it invokes either diversity of citizenship or federal question. If it does, the claim can be heard by the federal court. But what if it does not? What if we have such an additional claim in a federal court case and this additional claim does not invoke diversity and does not invoke federal question? Then—and only then—do we think about supplemental jurisdiction. Supplemental jurisdiction allows a federal court to hear non-diversity, non-federal claims—claims that by themselves could never go to federal court.

Supplemental jurisdiction is proper only if the claim being joined—the non-federal, non-diversity claim—is so closely related to the claim that got the case into federal court that they can be considered part of the same "case." The leading case is *United Mine Workers v. Gibbs*, 383 U.S. 715 (1966), a case arising from a labor dispute regarding coal mining in Appalachia. P, a citizen of Tennessee, sued D, which was also a citizen of Tennessee. P asserted two claims. Claim 1 was for violation of federal labor law and thus invoked federal question jurisdiction. That got the case into federal court. Claim 2, however, was for violation of state law. Claim 2 could not invoke federal question (because it arose under state law) and could not invoke diversity (because P and D were citizens of Tennessee). So Claim 2, by itself, could never have gone to federal court.

Nonetheless, the Court held that Claim 2 invoked supplemental jurisdiction (what was, when *Gibbs* was decided, called "pendent" jurisdiction). It did so because it was part of the same case as Claim 1, which had gotten the case into federal court as an initial matter. According to *Gibbs*, claims comprise part of the same case if they share a "common nucleus of operative fact" so that we reasonably would expect them to be tried together. The claims in *Gibbs* easily met this test because they arose from the same labor dispute at the same place. We will see in Chapter 8 that many Federal Rules permit joinder of claims if they arise from the "same transaction or occurrence" (T/O) as the underlying dispute. Here is some good news: claims that arise from the same T/O always satisfy the *Gibbs* test. *Gibbs* is even broader than T/O. It will grant supplemental jurisdiction over claims that have a mere "loose factual connection" with the claim that got the case into federal court initially.

Supplemental jurisdiction developed in case law. Congress codified it in § 1367. Section 1367(a) grants supplemental jurisdiction to all claims that are part of the same Article III case as a claim that got the case into federal court. Every court agrees that this codifies the result in *Gibbs*. Accordingly, claims that share a common nucleus of operative fact with the underlying claim (the claim that invoked either diversity of citizenship or federal question jurisdiction) will invoke supplemental jurisdiction under § 1367(a).

The last sentence of § 1367(a) provides that this is true even if the supplemental claim is asserted by or against an additional party. For example, in *Gibbs*, suppose P sued two defendants, D-1 and D-2. Claim 1 was asserted against D-1 and Claim 2 was asserted against D-2. Claim 1, as in *Gibbs*, invokes federal question jurisdiction, while Claim 2 does not invoke diversity or federal question. The claims share a common nucleus of operative fact, however, which means that § 1367(a) grants supplemental jurisdiction over Claim 2.

Congress needed to cut back on the grant of § 1367(a) to ensure that supplemental jurisdiction would not eviscerate the complete diversity rule and inundate the federal courts with cases.

It did so in § 1367(b). Read the provision carefully, and note three things.

First, § 1367(b) applies only in diversity of citizenship cases. It does not apply in cases that got into federal court through federal question jurisdiction.

Second, § 1367(b) denies supplemental jurisdiction in diversity cases only over claims asserted by plaintiffs. It does not apply to claims asserted by defendants.

Third, § 1367(b) applies only in diversity cases to *certain types of claims by plaintiffs*. Specifically, it denies supplemental jurisdiction over claims (1) by plaintiffs against parties joined under Federal Rule 14, 19, 20, and 24, (2) by Federal Rule 19 plaintiffs, and (3) by absentees seeking to intervene as plaintiffs under Federal Rule 24. We discuss each of these Federal Rules in Chapter 8, which addresses joinder. There, we will revisit supplemental jurisdiction in the context of the various joinder provisions. For now, let's try two hypotheticals to hone the application of § 1367(a) and (b).

> Example: *Gibbs* was decided 24 years before § 1367 was passed. How would *Gibbs* be decided under § 1367? First, does § 1367(a) grant supplemental jurisdiction over Claim 2 in that case? Yes. Claim 2 shared a common nucleus of operative fact with Claim 1, which invoked federal question jurisdiction. Second, does § 1367(b) deny supplemental jurisdiction? No. Section 1367(b) is irrelevant. It applies only to cases that initially invoked diversity jurisdiction. This case initially invoked federal question jurisdiction, so § 1367(b) does not apply.
>
> Example: P, a citizen of Utah, sues D, a citizen of Wyoming, for $150,000 damages arising from a car wreck between the two. D files a "compulsory counterclaim"

against P in the case. As we will see in Chapter 8, § C, this is a claim by D against P that arises from the same T/O as P's claim. The counterclaim is for $50,000. Note that the counterclaim does not invoke federal question jurisdiction (because car wrecks are state-law claims) and it does not invoke diversity jurisdiction (because it does not exceed $75,000). After explaining that to your professor, you would assess whether the counterclaim invokes supplemental jurisdiction. First, § 1367(a) grants supplemental jurisdiction. The counterclaim arose from the same T/O as the underlying claim, so it meets the common nucleus of operative fact test of *Gibbs*. Second, § 1367(b) does not deny supplemental jurisdiction. Why? Even though this is a diversity case, remember that § 1367(b) only applies to claims by a plaintiff. The counterclaim is asserted by a defendant.

In *Gibbs*, the Supreme Court held that courts have discretion to decline supplemental jurisdiction in certain situations. For example, if the claim that got the case into federal court initially were dismissed early in the case, the court might refuse to exercise supplemental jurisdiction. So in *Gibbs*, if the court had dismissed Claim 1 for failure to state a claim, and had done so before it had invested much time in the case, it would probably dismiss Claim 2. Congress attempted to codify this and other discretionary factors from *Gibbs* in § 1367(c).

E. Removal from State to Federal Court

So far, the choice of forum has been made by P. Removal gives D a voice in determining where the case will be heard. It allows a defendant who was sued in state court to "remove" the case to federal court. Thus, it transfers the case from a state trial court to a federal trial court. Technically, the word "transfer" applies to changes of venue within the same judicial system (so we will speak of transfer from one federal district to another federal district in Chapter 4, § B). So we use the term of art "remove" instead.

Removal is governed by 28 U.S.C. §§ 1441, 1446, and 1447. Together, those statutes provide a series of rules. We will review the major ones. Removal is a one-way street: it goes only from state trial court to a federal trial court. There is no such thing as removing a case from federal to state court. If removal is improper, the federal court will "remand" the case back to state court.

D does not need permission to remove. D files a "notice of removal" in the appropriate federal court. That document is signed under Rule 11 (Chapter 5, last paragraph of § A) and states the subject matter jurisdiction basis on which removal is made. It must be accompanied with all documents that have been served upon D by that point in the state litigation. D then serves a copy of the notice of removal and other documents on P. After this, she files a copy of the notice in the state court. That filing divests the state court of jurisdiction.

As a general rule, defendant can remove if the case could have been brought in federal court. In other words, she can remove if the case meets the requirements of diversity of citizenship or of federal question jurisdiction. So with removal, D can override P's choice of forum because she would prefer to have the federal court hear a case that falls within federal subject matter jurisdiction.

There are two important exceptions to this general rule. Both exceptions apply only in diversity of citizenship cases; they do not apply in federal question cases. First, the case cannot be removed if any defendant is a citizen of the forum in which P filed the case. This "in-state defendant" rule makes sense. If D is a local citizen, she (in theory) need not fear the bias of state courts, so she need not gain access to the federal forum. Second, generally, D cannot remove a case more than one year after it was filed in state court.

This timing provision can give us some trouble, because we have to be aware of an even more important timing rule. D must remove no later than 30 days after she is served with the document that first makes the case removable. Almost always, this means within 30 days after being served with process in the case. Why? Because most removable cases will be removable at the outset. The requirements for diversity of citizenship or for federal question jurisdiction will be met initially, and D must remove within 30 days of service of process on her. So the one-year provision we noted in the preceding paragraph usually will be irrelevant. But some cases are not removable initially. They become removable later.

> Example: P, a citizen of New Jersey, sues two defendants: D-1 (a citizen of Alabama) and D-2 (a citizen of Pennsylvania). She asserts a state-law claim that exceeds $75,000. She sues in state court in Pennsylvania. Can D-1 and D-2 remove the case to federal court?

We want to say yes, because this is a case that could have been brought in federal court. Why? It meets all the requirements for diversity jurisdiction: P is of diverse citizenship from both defendants and the amount in controversy exceeds $75,000. But then we run into the first exception we saw two paragraphs above the Example: you cannot remove a diversity case if any defendant is a citizen of the forum. Here, we are in a Pennsylvania state court and one of the defendants is a citizen of Pennsylvania. This "in-state defendant" defeats removal.[6]

---

[6] Quick quiz: suppose P's case alleged that the defendants violated her rights under federal law? Then the case would invoke federal question jurisdiction and the

But suppose P voluntarily dismisses the claim against D-2. The case *just became removable*. Why? Because we still meet the requirements for diversity of citizenship jurisdiction and now there is no in-state defendant. Here, the 30-day rule is relevant: the remaining defendant (D-1) must remove no later than 30 days after being served with the voluntary dismissal of the D-2 (that is the document that first made this case removable). Now, however, we may run into the other timing provision—we cannot remove a diversity case more than one year after it was filed in state court. So if more than one year has passed since the case was filed, D-2 cannot remove.

This is a stupid rule. It allows plaintiffs to join a defendant who defeats removal, wait a year, and then dismiss the claim against that person. That leaves the other defendant unable to remove. In 2012, Congress moderated the rule slightly. Now, under § 1446(c)(1), a defendant can remove a diversity case more than one year after the case was filed if the federal court finds that P acted in bad faith to prevent removal. This is likely to be a tough standard to meet.

Congress also acted in 2012 to clarify another timing question regarding removal. It has always been clear that *all* defendants who have been served with the document that makes the case removable must join in the notice of removal. Let's say the case is (as most are) removable at the outset—it meets the requirements for diversity of citizenship or federal question jurisdiction. The case is filed in state court on May 10. Let's say there are two defendants. D-1 and D-2 are served with process on May 15. Under the rule of unanimity, both defendants must join in the notice of

---

fact that we have an in-state defendant is irrelevant. Remember, the in-state defendant rule applies only in diversity cases.

removal no later than 30 days after May 15. If only one of the two wants to remove, the case cannot be removed.

Now let's say the case is filed on May 10. D-1 is served with process on May 15. D-2 is not yet served with process. Can D-1 alone remove? Yes. She is the only defendant who has been *served*—the 30 days runs from when you are *served* with the document that makes the case removable. So D-1 may remove the case to federal court. D-2 need not join in the removal because D-2 has not yet been served with process.

Now let's say D-1 does not remove within 30 days. On July 30, D-2 is served with process. For years, courts could not agree on whether the 30 days for removal started running again with the service on D-2. Some courts said no—and thus that D-1's failure to remove estopped D-2 from trying to do so. But Congress resolved the matter the other way. It is now clear that the 30 days runs anew from service on D-2. The rule of unanimity still applies, so D-2 will have to get D-1 to join the notice of removal. They have 30 days after service on D-2 on July 30 in which to do so.

Defendants cannot remove to just any federal court they like. Removal is proper *only* to the federal district that embraces the state court in which the case was filed. So if the case was filed in state court in San Diego, it can be removed only to the federal district for the Southern District of California, which embraces that great city (my hometown—Go Padres!).

P might move to remand the case to state court on two bases. First, if the case does not invoke federal subject matter jurisdiction, it *must* be remanded. Accordingly, there is no time limit on seeking remand for lack of subject matter jurisdiction. In fact, the court itself must remand if there is no subject matter jurisdiction, even in the absence of a motion. Because D is invoking federal jurisdiction, she has the burden of showing that the requirements are satisfied. The second basis for seeking remand is that D did something wrong procedurally. For example, perhaps she failed to sign the notice of removal. P must make a motion to remand based upon procedural issues no later than 30 days after the notice of removal was filed. Failure to do so waives the defect, and the case stays in federal court (assuming, or course, that there is federal subject matter jurisdiction).

CHAPTER 4

Selecting a Forum: Venue, Transfer, and Forum Non Conveniens

A. The General Venue Provisions

Personal jurisdiction told us that the plaintiff (P) may sue the defendant (D) in a particular state (or states). Subject matter jurisdiction told us whether that case would go to federal court or to state court in that state. Venue tells us exactly where (geographically) the case will be filed in the chosen judicial system. States usually prescribe venue rules by county. In federal court, venue tells us exactly which (of 94) federal districts may hear our case. 28 U.S.C. § 1390(a) defines venue as the "geographic specification of the proper court or courts for the litigation of a civil action that is within the subject matter jurisdiction of the district courts. . . ."

Venue provisions are intended to ensure that litigation is held in a relatively convenient place. The most common provisions permit venue where D resides and where a substantial part of the claim arose. These will usually be convenient places for litigation. Certainly, D can rarely complain if sued where she resides. And laying venue where the relevant events occurred will usually mean that witnesses will be readily available.

In the federal system, as noted, venue is keyed to federal districts. Many states comprise a single district, such as the District of Arizona or the District of South Carolina. Some states consist of two districts, some of three, and three states (California, Texas, and New York) have four districts. The districts have boring geographic names, such as the Northern District of Florida and the Middle District of Pennsylvania. Congress determines how many districts will be established in each state and what parts of the state are assigned to each district. Venue in federal civil cases is governed entirely by statute.[1] If P files suit in an improper venue, D must make a timely objection, or else he waives the defense. A court has no duty to raise the fact that venue is improper. (This is different from subject matter jurisdiction, which a federal court is required to raise on its own.)

The general venue statute is 28 U.S.C. § 1391(b). It governs venue in virtually every civil case filed initially in federal court, whether based upon diversity of citizenship or federal question jurisdiction. Section 1391(b) gives P two general alternatives for laying venue: (1) where D resides ("residential" venue) or where a substantial part of the events underlying the claim took place ("transactional" venue). A third option—"fallback" venue under § 1391(b)(3)—will almost never work, as we will see below.

---

[1] Until 2012, there was a significant common law component to federal venue. Specifically, if a claim was "local"—which was defined as one relating to ownership of or injury to land—venerable case law required that venue be laid in the district in which the land lay. All other actions were "transitory," to which statutory venue provisions applied. In 2012, the distinction between local and transitory cases was abolished in the federal courts. See 28 U.S.C. § 1391(a)(2).

Residential Venue

Do not be misled by the statutory language for the first option, found in § 1391(b)(1). Though it speaks of laying venue in any district where "any" defendant resides, the rest of the provision modifies it. Section 1391(b)(1) means that venue is proper in any district where *all* defendants reside. As a sub-rule, if all defendants reside in different districts of the forum state, venue is proper against all in a district where one of them resides.

> Example: P sues two defendants: D-1 (who resides in the District of Nevada) and D-2 (who resides in the Eastern District of California). Venue is not proper in either of those districts under § 1391(b)(1). Indeed, no district in the United States will satisfy § 1391(b)(1) on these facts, because there is no district in which all defendants reside.

> Example: P sues two defendants: D-1 (who resides in the Southern District of New York) and D-2 (who resides in the Western District of New York). Both defendants may be sued in one case either in the Southern or the Western District of New York. Venue would not be proper under § 1391(b)(1), however, in the Eastern District of New York or the Northern District of New York.

Where do litigants "reside" for venue purposes? Under § 1391(c)(1), a human resides in the district in which she is domiciled. As we saw in Chapter 3, § B, a person can only have one domicile at a time. Thus, for venue purposes, she can reside only in one district at a time. Equating residence with domicile does not comport with the common understanding of residence. For example, a college student who is domiciled in Missouri but attends college for four years in Ohio might think she "resides" in

Ohio (at least during the school year). But (for venue purposes) she does not; her residence is the district of her domicile.

Section 1391(c)(2) defines the residence of entities, such as corporations and partnerships. Such defendants reside in all districts in which they would be subject to personal jurisdiction for the suit at hand. So while a human can only have one district of residence, a business might have several—because it resides in each district in which it is subject to personal jurisdiction.[2]

Transactional Venue

Under § 1391(b)(2), venue may be laid in any district where "a substantial part of the events or omissions giving rise to the claim occurred." There may be more than one district that qualifies under this provision.

> Example: Manufacturer designs and builds a product in the Eastern District of Tennessee. It sells and ships the product to P, who resides in the Western District of Missouri. The product is defective and injures P in the latter district. Both the Eastern District of Tennessee and the Western District of Missouri are likely proper venues because substantial parts of the events underlying the tort occurred in each—the faulty design or manufacture in one and injury in the other.

"Fallback" Venue

Section 1391(b)(3) seems too good to be true. It allows venue in *any* district in which *any* defendant is subject to personal jurisdiction. So why not just use § 1391(b)(3) every time? Look at

---

[2]   The statute also defines the residence of such businesses when they are plaintiffs. That is irrelevant for us, because § 1391(b) does not allow venue where P resides. It is in the statute because some specialized venue provisions allow venue where P resides. We do not address those statutes in Civil Procedure.

the terms carefully. Section 1391(b)(3) applies only if there is *no district in the United States that can satisfy either § 1391(b)(1) or § 1391(b)(2)*. In other words, the fallback provision applies only if there is no district anywhere in the United States where all defendants reside or where a substantial part of the claim arose. Only if the claim arose overseas will this be possible. If any substantial part of the events underlying the claim arose in the United States, there will be a district satisfying § 1391(b)(2). So § 1391(b)(3) almost never applies.

B. Transfer of Venue

Each judicial system provides a mechanism for transferring a case from one place in that system to another place in the same system. Usually, transfer is permitted either to fix a venue problem or to ensure that litigation proceeds in a more convenient locale. So when P lays venue in an improper place, that court may order transfer to a proper venue. This is better than requiring P to re-file in the proper place. Sometimes, the original venue is technically proper but, on the facts of the case, not as convenient as another venue in the system. Transfer may get the case to the more appropriate place.

Transfer can be ordered only to another court in the same judicial system. So a case in state court in Omaha, Nebraska may be transferred to a state court in Lincoln, Nebraska. But a case in state court in Omaha cannot be transferred to a state court in Iowa; those states are separate sovereigns. In contrast, the federal judicial system exists in every state. So a case in federal district court in Nebraska can be transferred to a federal district court in Iowa.

The Federal Transfer Statutes

In the federal system, there are two general transfer statutes: 28 U.S.C. § 1404(a) and § 1406(a). Under each, if transfer is ordered, the case goes from the "transferor" district to the "transferee" district. Now, why do we need two transfer statutes?

Section 1404(a) applies when the transferor district is a *proper venue*. It permits transfer to another district for "the convenience of parties and witnesses, in the interest of justice." Even though the transferor is a proper venue, another district might be more convenient. The party seeking transfer (usually D) has the burden of convincing the court to override P's original choice of venue. She will attempt to show that the alternative court is simply a better and more convenient location for the litigation. Though the phrase does not appear in any statute, many people summarize the idea by saying that the alternative forum is the "center of gravity."

In deciding whether to order transfer, the court looks to a series of "public" and "private" interest factors. Public factors include the local interest in the controversy, the interest in having trial in a forum familiar with the law that will govern the dispute. Private factors focus on convenience of parties and witnesses, including availability of subpoenas for unwilling witnesses and access to relevant records. Courts have enormous discretion in deciding whether to order transfer, and their decisions are rarely reversed on appeal.

Section 1406(a) applies when the transferor district is an *improper venue*. It gives the court an option: the original federal court may dismiss the case (after all, venue is improper) or transfer "in the interest of justice." Usually, a court will transfer to avoid making P start all over in a proper court.

The Transferee District

Section 1404(a) and § 1406(a) require that the transferee district be a place where the case "could" or "might" have been brought. In *Hoffman v. Blaski,* 363 U.S. 335 (1960), the Court held that this language means that the transferee must (1) be a proper venue and (2) have personal jurisdiction over D. Not only that, these two things must be true independently—that is, without any waiver by the defendant. Though *Hoffman* was a § 1404(a) case, the courts have applied it to § 1406(a) as well.

> Example: P sues D in the District of Minnesota. D moves to transfer to the District of Hawaii. D admits that the District of Hawaii is not a proper venue and does not have personal jurisdiction over him, but agrees to waive these objections. Under *Hoffman*, transfer cannot be ordered. The transferee must be a proper venue and have personal jurisdiction over D independent of any waiver by D.

Personal Jurisdiction in the Transferor Court

In *Goldlawr, Inc. v. Heiman,* 369 U.S. 463 (1962), the Court held that a § 1406(a) transfer was proper even though the transferor court lacked personal jurisdiction over D. The courts have generally adopted the holding for § 1404(a) transfers as well.

Choice of Law Issues

Every state has its own "choice of law" doctrine. The purpose of that doctrine is to determine what law to apply when resolving a dispute. It may seem odd, but it is routine for courts to apply the law of other jurisdictions. For example, suppose P is injured at home in Oregon by a defective product manufactured in Oklahoma. P sues the manufacturer in Oregon. Oregon choice of law rules will determine whether the tort law of Oregon or of

Oklahoma (or of some other place) will govern in the case. You will study choice of law doctrine in an upper-level course called Conflict of Laws. For now, we need to know that each state has rules on the subject, and that the rules can vary from state to state.

In diversity of citizenship cases, the federal court must use the "choice of law" rules of the state in which the court sits. So a federal court in Oregon, deciding a diversity case, uses Oregon choice of law doctrine to determine what law will apply. What happens when the case is transferred? In *Van Dusen v. Barrack*, 376 U.S. 612 (1964), a § 1404(a) case, the Court held that the choice of law rules of the transferor court apply in the transferee court. It reasoned that a transfer under § 1404(a) should result only in a change of courtrooms and not a change in the governing law. So if the case were transferred under § 1404(a) to a federal district in Oklahoma, the Oklahoma federal judge would apply Oregon choice of law doctrine.

In *Ferens v. John Deere Co.*, 494 U.S. 516 (1990), the Court extended *Van Dusen* to a § 1404(a) transfer sought by the *plaintiff*. Many people criticize *Ferens* because it allows a plaintiff to sue in one place, "capture" the choice of law rules of that place, and then have the case transferred to a more convenient venue. There are limits, however, to the plaintiff's ability to use transfer to capture favorable choice of law doctrine. Specifically, *Van Dusen* should not apply to § 1406(a) transfers or to any transfer effected under *Goldlawr*. By definition, plaintiff in such cases has sued in an improper place—a place that is an improper venue or that lacks personal jurisdiction over the defendant. It would be unfair to permit the plaintiff to capture the choice of law rules of such an improper forum.[3]

---

[3]   In *Atlantic Marine Const. Co. v. U.S. District Court*, 134 S.Ct. 568 (2013), the Court held that *Van Dusen* does not apply in a § 1404(a) transfer to a district

C. Forum Non Conveniens

Like transfer under § 1404(a), *forum non conveniens* is relevant when some other court is a substantially more appropriate location for litigation than the present one. But here, instead of transferring the case to that "center of gravity" court, the court dismisses the case. (Instead of dismissing, the court may "stay" the case, which means it will be held in abeyance, with no litigation taking place.) Why would a court take such a seemingly harsh step? Because transfer is impossible! The better court is in a different judicial system, so transfer is not an option. So a state court in Nebraska may dismiss a case if it is convinced that the litigation should proceed in state court Iowa. By dismissing, the court tells P to file a new case in Iowa.

Usually, the more appropriate court is in a foreign country (to which transfer is obviously impossible). The leading case is *Piper Aircraft Co. v. Reyno*, 454 U.S. 235 (1981). The case involved a plane crash in Scotland, in which all passengers and crew were killed. The victims and their next-of-kin were Scottish. The airline and pilot were Scottish. The maintenance crew was Scottish. The plane was manufactured, however, in Pennsylvania, using propellers made in Ohio. The Supreme Court held that suit against the American manufacturers in federal court in Pennsylvania should be dismissed for *forum non conveniens*. The center of gravity of the dispute was Scotland, and the case should be dismissed in favor of litigation in that country.

The determination of whether the other court is the center of gravity is based upon the same public and private factors that are relevant for transfer under § 1404(a), discussed in the previous

prescribed in the parties' forum selection clause. The fact that the parties provided in their contract that any litigation should take place in a particular location does not render improper other venues that are allowed under the relevant venue statutes. But the clause can be enforced by transferring to the chosen district.

section. With *forum non conveniens*, however, the moving party has an especially strong burden of proof, because here the result granting the motion is not transfer, but dismissal.

There is another important step in *forum non conveniens* analysis. The court must be convinced that the center of gravity court is "available and adequate." It would be unfair to dismiss American litigation if there were no adequate judicial forum in the other country. Plaintiffs will argue that foreign courts are inadequate because they rarely adopt cutting-edge tort theories and often do not permit recovery for things like pain and suffering and emotional distress. Many countries do not allow broad discovery or trial by jury. The Court has routinely rejected such arguments. In *Piper*, it held that the foreign court is adequate unless P can show "the remedy provided by the alternative forum is so clearly inadequate or unsatisfactory that it is no remedy at all." Very few plaintiffs can make such a showing. The result of *forum non conveniens* dismissals is often the end of the matter, because many plaintiffs decide not proceed in the foreign country.

Forum non conveniens orders are often conditioned on the defendant's waiving some potential defense in the foreign court. For instance, an American court might dismiss only if the defendant agrees to submit to personal jurisdiction or to waive any statute of limitations defense or to submit to American-style discovery in the foreign country. Defendants are usually eager to do so to avoid litigation in the United States, which is generally far more pro-plaintiff than courts in other lands.

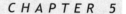

CHAPTER 5

The Litigation Process: Early Stages

A. Pleadings and Motions

Pleadings are documents in which the parties set forth claims and defenses. There are two general pleadings: the complaint by the plaintiff (P) and the answer by the defendant (D). These are filed with the court and served on the other party. Pleadings are to be contrasted with *motions*, which are requests for a court order. Any time a party asks the court for an order—say, to transfer to another district or to require the other party to do something—she will make a motion. We focus here on motions under Rule 12.

The Complaint

P commences the case by filing the *complaint*. This document must contain three elements, of which the first and third are usually easy to satisfy. Rule 8(a)(1) requires a statement of the grounds of subject matter jurisdiction, so P must allege facts that show either diversity of citizenship or federal question jurisdiction. Rule 8(a)(3) requires that P make a request for judgment—tell the court what relief she seeks (such as damages to compensate for harm, or restitution of property improperly held by D, or an injunction to require D to stop infringing P's copyright).

The big requirement is in Rule 8(a)(2): P must make a "short and plain statement of the claim, showing that [she] is entitled to relief." There is no sense burdening D to engage in further litigation (such as filing an answer and producing materials in discovery) if P cannot allege a claim. D raises the issue by filing a motion to dismiss for failure to state a claim under Rule 12(b)(6)(in some states the function is performed by a "demurrer"). The court then assesses whether the complaint is *legally* and *factually* sufficient. It does so based on what P alleged. It does *not* consider evidence of what really happened. For this motion, we are willing to assume that what P alleged is true. The court asks, basically, "if what P says is true, would P win a judgment?" If the answer is no, the case fails to get past the "pleading stage" and does not belong in the litigation stream.

Assessing a complaint's *legal* sufficiency is a matter of researching the state of the jurisdiction's substantive law.

> Example: P alleged: "I told the defendant to have a nice day and she did not respond, which made me feel bad." Even if these allegations turned out to be true, P cannot win. There is no state in which these facts constitute an actionable tort (not even California). The complaint is legally insufficient.

The tougher issue is whether the complaint is *factually* sufficient. The law recognizes a claim here, but has P alleged enough to justify going forward in litigation? We have long had a debate about how much detail should be required. The "code pleading" system, which is still followed in a few states, requires P to state "facts constituting a cause of action." Courts could not agree on what constituted "facts" (as opposed to "conclusions") and tended to require P to plead a great deal of factual detail. Without discovery, some plaintiffs did not have access to factual detail. And without being able to allege a claim, they could not get access to discovery. So detailed factual pleading had the effect of keeping some plaintiffs out of litigation.

The Federal Rules, promulgated in 1938, ushered in a new approach. The goal of Rule 8(a)(2) was to lower the pleading barrier, to make it easier to get into the litigation stream. The drafters consciously avoided the word "facts," because it implied a need for detail. Under the Federal Rules, P need merely plead enough detail to put D on notice of what she was being sued for. It came to be known as "notice pleading." But this system, some argued, made it too easy for plaintiffs to get past the pleading stage and to subject defendants to the burdens and expense of discovery. Some lower federal courts tried to impose "heightened" pleading requirements, at least in some types of cases. The Supreme Court rejected these efforts and stuck with Rule 8(a)(2).

Surprisingly, the Court changed course with *Bell Atlantic Corp. v. Twombly*, 550 U.S. 544 (2009) and *Ashcroft v. Iqbal*, 556 U.S. 662 (2007) (together called *Twiqbal*). In these cases, the Court raised the pleading barrier for plaintiffs. The cases establish three principles for determining whether P has stated a claim. First, the court is to ignore P's "conclusions of law." This instruction is problematic. For instance, is the allegation "defendant drove her car negligently" a conclusion of law (or is it a statement of fact)?

Second, the court is to look at P's "allegations of fact." This is odd because, as we just said, the drafters of Rule 8 expressly avoided the word "facts." Third, the court is to determine whether the "facts" alleged state a "plausible" claim. A "possible" claim is not enough—it must be "plausible." In making this assessment, the judge is to be guided by her own experience and common sense. But "plausible" is not found in Rule 8. And asking each judge to use her own common sense is an invitation to subjectivity.

The *Twiqbal* cases have generated a stunning amount of law review commentary and debate. Some studies suggest that the cases have not had a profound effect on dismissal rates, but most observers agree that more study is needed.

When a court grants a Rule 12(b)(6) motion to dismiss, it often does so "without prejudice," which gives P a chance to try again. At some point, however, the court may conclude that P simply cannot state a claim. Then, the court will dismiss "with prejudice," which ends the matter.

Defendant's Response

How does D respond to the complaint? She has a choice: within 21 days after being served with process, she may respond by motion or by answer. (If she waived service under Rule 4(d), she gets 60 days from the date on which P mailed the materials to her.) Again, a motion is not a pleading, but is a request for a court order. Three subsections of Rule 12 permit motions. One, Rule 12(e), permits the motion for more definite statement. These are rare, and are proper only when the complaint is unintelligible. Two, Rule 12(f) permits any party to bring a motion to strike, which asks the court to order that parts of a document (or even the entire document) be stricken. This motion is appropriate, for example, to remove scandalous or irrelevant material from a document.

The third provision—Rule 12(b)—is the most important. Rule 12(b) lists seven defenses and allows D to raise any of them either in a motion (to dismiss) or in the answer. The defenses are: (1) lack of subject matter jurisdiction, (2) lack of personal jurisdiction, (3) improper venue, (4) improper process (meaning a problem with the documents constituting process, which are the summons and a copy of the complaint), (5) improper service of process (the documents were fine but were not served properly), (6) failure to state a claim on which relief can be granted (we discussed this immediately above), and (7) failure to join an "indispensable" party under Rule 19 (discussed in Chapter 8, § D).

The fact that D may raise these defenses either by motion or by answer opens the door for a mistake that will result in waiver of a defense. D must be careful to abide by Rules 12(g) and (h), which impose timing requirements. The provisions are not all that clear, so let's cut to the chase. Here is what they mean:

- Defenses in Rule 12(b)(2), (3), (4), and (5) must be asserted in D's first Rule 12 response. So whatever D chooses to do first under Rule 12—either to serve an answer or a motion—these defenses must be in that first Rule 12 response. If they are not included in that response, the defenses are waived.

- Defenses in Rules 12(b)(6) and (7) may be asserted for the first time anytime through trial. So these do not have to be put in the first Rule 12 response. They are not waived, so long as D asserts them no later than at trial. These could not be raised for the first time on appeal (because that is after trial).

- The defense in Rule 12(b)(1)—lack of subject matter jurisdiction—can be raised for the first time any time in the case. Subject matter jurisdiction is never waived. It can be raised for the first time even on appeal.

When the exam rolls around, everyone will know these rules. Remember, however, that the grade is not based on whether you can state the rules. It is based on whether you recognize the rules on a fact pattern. So be on the lookout any time you see a D making a response under Rule 12!

> Example: P sues D. D brings a motion to dismiss for lack of subject matter jurisdiction. The court denies the motion. Now D moves to dismiss for lack of personal jurisdiction. In fact, assume that D has absolutely no contacts with the forum state.
>
> D has waived the defense. It does not matter that she has no contacts with the forum. She has waived the personal jurisdiction defense. Whenever you see D make her *first Rule 12 response*—which means an answer or a Rule 12 motion—watch out for waiver. She must include in that first response all defenses in Rule 12(b)(2), (3), (4), and (5). If she does not, the defenses are waived.

Instead of making a motion under Rule 12, D may simply answer. An answer is a pleading. In the answer, D will do two things. First, she responds to the allegations of the complaint under Rule 8(b). This means D will go through the complaint allegation by allegation and respond—either by admitting or denying. If she lacks sufficient information to admit or to deny (and such information is not in her control), she may so state in the answer, and this will be treated as a denial. Allegations that D properly denies are said to be "joined." Those factual issues are contested, and will be the subject of discovery and adjudication. Allegations that D expressly admits (or fails to deny properly) are deemed admitted.

Second, D will set forth affirmative defenses under Rule 8(c). With an affirmative defense, D raises a new fact—one that, if true, will entitle D to escape liability. An affirmative defense essentially says "even if I did what P says, P cannot win." For example, P cannot win because the statute of limitations has run, or the contract was not in writing, as it should have been under the Statute of Frauds. In general, affirmative defenses may be waived if they are not set forth in the answer.

Rule 11

Rule 11(a), which is a bulwark of professional responsibility, requires a lawyer to sign all documents (except discovery documents, as to which Rule 26(g) requires much the same thing). By signing, she certifies under Rule 11(b) that she has made a reasonable investigation and (1) that the document is not presented for an improper purpose, (2) that it is warranted by law, (3) that factual allegations have evidentiary support and (4) that denials of factual allegations have evidentiary support. Rule 11 is intended to ensure that lawyers do appropriate homework before making an assertion to the court.

Next Stages

If P's complaint survives the Rule 12(b) gauntlet, the case proceeds to the next stage of litigation, discovery. These stages are not hermetically sealed—the court does not announce one day "we are moving from the pleading stage to the discovery stage." In fact, there may be more pleadings. Rule 15 gives parties the right to amend their pleadings in certain circumstances, and to ask for "leave" to amend virtually anytime. But at some point, we will pass from the preliminaries—the questions of whether we are in the right court, whether P has stated a claim—and move on.

B. Discovery

Our adversarial system of justice depends upon each side's presenting the facts supporting her contentions to a neutral fact-finder (often the jury). The fact-finder determines what really happened—was the traffic light red, did D breach the contract, did

P suffer harm, did the automobile brakes fail? We do not believe in "trial by ambush." That is, we do not want a party to be able to present something at trial that surprises the other party. If that were allowed, the outcome would depend more on the facile reaction of the lawyer than on the facts. We want to know the truth. And to that end, we permit each party to "discover" what the other side knows.

Discovery Tools

There have always been five devices by which parties engage in discovery: the deposition, interrogatories, requests to produce, medical examinations, and requests for admission. All five can be used to get information from a party to the case, but only two—the deposition and the request to produce—can be used to obtain information from nonparties.

The first discovery tool is the *deposition.* Here, the person being "deposed" testifies orally under oath, just as she would if she were a witness at trial. But here, her testimony is not given in the courtroom and no judge or jury is present. Depositions are taken in somebody's office. The deponent responds to questions asked by the lawyers for all parties. The questions and answers are recorded by a stenographer and usually transcribed into booklet form. The deponent reviews the booklet, corrects any errors, and signs the transcript under oath. Rule 30 provides the details for taking depositions.

Depositions under Rule 30 are useful in part because they are "live."[1] Good lawyers learn how to gauge the deponent's reaction

---

[1]   What we are discussing is the deposition on oral examination. In contrast, Rule 31 provides for deposition upon written question. Here, the questions to be asked are written out in advance and read by the court reporter. The lawyers for the parties do not attend and thus lack the ability to react "live" to any bombshell information revealed by the deponent. Rule 31 is not widely used, but offers a less expensive alternative to the deposition on oral questions.

to questions and to pursue topics as the deposition evolves. One may even uncover the "smoking gun"—a major break in the case. But depositions are expensive because they are so time intensive for the lawyers. The lawyers will want to be prepared for the deposition, so usually will take them after learning preliminary facts through interrogatories and required disclosures under Rule 26(a)(1).

A party may take the deposition of anyone, party or non-party. The lawyer taking a deposition of a non-party should have the deponent subpoenaed under Rule 45. A subpoena is a court order compelling the non-party to attend at the stated time and place. Once she is under subpoena, if the deponent fails to attend, the court may hold her in contempt. Party deponents need not be subpoenaed. Merely sending them a notice of deposition, setting a reasonable time and place for the deposition, will secure their attendance.

The second discovery device is *interrogatories* under Rule 33. These are written questions, answered in writing under oath. They can be sent only to parties, and not to non-parties. The party has 30 days in which to respond, so one rarely finds a "smoking gun" in interrogatories. Still, they are useful to discover background information and to force the other party to give details about her claims or defenses.

The third discovery tool is the *request to produce* under Rule 34. This requires the respondent to allow access to documents, electronically stored information (ESI), and tangible things. The discovering party then gets to review these things and make copies or run tests on the things (such as the allegedly malfunctioning widget). This tool is available to get such information from parties or non-parties. Note, however, that it is only enforceable against a non-party under Rule 34(c) if the request is accompanied by a subpoena. Often, the function of a Rule 34 request is combined with a deposition of a non-party. The non-party could be served with a *subpoena duces tecum*, which requires the non-party to attend the deposition and to bring the requested documents, ESI, and things with her.

The fourth discovery tool is the *medical examination* under Rule 35. This permits a party to force someone to undergo a relevant examination by an appropriate health care professional. For example, if P claims physical injuries, D will probably want to have her doctor examine P. Rule 35 provides significant protection for the person to be examined. A medical exam is available only upon court order, and the order is not easy to get. The discovering party must demonstrate that the condition to be examined—which might be physical or mental—is relevant to the case and that there is "good cause" to order the exam.

A Rule 35 exam can only be ordered of a party or someone in the "custody or legal control" of a party. For example, suppose litigation concerns alleged injuries to a minor. The child is not a party because she lacks legal capacity to sue or be sued. The child's parent sues on the child's behalf. D may seek a medical exam of the child because children are in the "custody or legal control" of their parents (at least in theory).

The fifth discovery device is the *request for admission* under Rule 36. These may be sent only to parties, and not to non-parties. They require the party to admit or deny specific factual statements. The responding party has 30 days in which to respond. For example, P in a car crash case could send to D a Rule 36 request requiring D to admit or deny that she had drunk alcohol within 10 minutes of the crash. If D does not deny the within 30 days, she is deemed to have admitted it.

In addition to these five discovery tools, in federal court the parties have "required" or "mandatory" disclosures under Rule 26(a). That provision requires each party to give information to the other parties at three points in the litigation—and to do so *without a request by a party*. The three types of mandatory disclosure are found in Rule 26(a)(1), 26(a)(2), and 26(a)(3).

Under Rule 26(a)(1) ("initial" required disclosures), each party must identify persons who have discoverable information that she may use to support her contentions on the merits in the case. In addition, she must describe or produce documents, ESI, and things that constitute discoverable material that she may use to support her contentions in the case. Moreover, P must provide a calculation of damages and D must identify any insurance she has which may cover all or part of the claims against her.

The other mandatory disclosure provisions are relevant later in the case. Rule 26(a)(2) requires identification of and information from expert witnesses whom the party will be using at trial. This usually becomes relevant late in the discovery phase of litigation, when we know who our expert witnesses will be. Rule 26(a)(3) are the "pretrial" mandatory disclosures, which come up after the parties have finished discovery and are getting ready for trial. Rule 26(b)(3) requires each party to set forth every contention it will raise at trial, including witnesses and evidence, in a memo, which is filed with the court.

Scope of Discovery

Now that we know the discovery tools, we need to determine what kind of information we can attempt to discover. The answer is found in Rule 26(b)(1), which allows discovery of any relevant, non-privileged information. In the course on Evidence, you will study what information may be admitted into evidence at trial. For example, in general, hearsay is not admissible, so a witness will not be permitted to testify at trial about what somebody told her. But the scope of discovery is broader, as shown by the provision in Rule 26(b)(1) that we may discover information "reasonably calculated to lead to the discovery of admissible evidence." So we may ask a witness in a deposition about what someone told him. That information may not be admissible when we get to trial but it is discoverable if it may lead to something admissible at trial. For instance, the witness might tell us that he was told that D had been drinking alcohol while driving the car that was involved in a collision.

Discovery is not without limits. First, there is no right to discover "privileged" information. "Privileged" is a term of art and raises another topic you will study in the Evidence course. In this sense, privilege refers to *confidential communications* between particular persons, such as lawyer and client, spouses, or clergyperson and parishioner. (There is no "bff" privilege, so unless you fall within one of these relationships, you and your bff can be made to divulge relevant convos and e-mails.) Because the law wants to promote honest and open communication between these persons, the content of these communications are not discoverable, no matter how relevant. Recognition of privilege obviously inhibits the search for truth, so the burden is on the party claiming privilege to assert it timely and with specificity.

Privilege attaches only to "confidential" communications between the specific types of persons. So if you are bowling with your lawyer and your hair stylist when you say to them "you know, lawyer, I did rob that bank after all"—you have a problem. The communication was not confidential between you and your lawyer, so it is not privileged.

Second, there is no right to discover what everyone calls "work product" (though the provision addressing it, Rule 26(b)(4), refers to "trial preparation materials"). This is material created "in anticipation of litigation" by a party or a representative of a party. It is protected from discovery to ensure that one party does not freeload off the work done by or for another party.

Example: Several people are injured when a fairground ride malfunctions. The operator of the ride, knowing that it will be sued, hires a private investigator to inspect the area and talk to witnesses. The investigator writes his findings in a memo to the operator. When plaintiffs sue the operator and request relevant documents, must the operator produce the report? No. It is work product because it was generated in anticipation of litigation. As long as the ride operator claims the work product protection timely and with specificity, it can refuse to produce the document.

Many people use the phrase "attorney work product." Indeed, in some states, material is only protected as work product if a lawyer prepared it. In federal court, however, the concept is broader. Under Rule 26(b)(4), work product can be generated by the party herself or by *any representative* of a party. Thus, in the Example, the memo was work product even though prepared not by a lawyer but by a private investigator. So in federal court, the concept is "work product," and not "attorney work product."

Work product protection is not absolute. So Rule 26(b)(4) would permit the plaintiffs in this case if they can show (1) substantial need for the information and (2) that they cannot without undue hardship get the equivalent of the information. For instance, if the private investigator spoke to eyewitnesses and those people cannot now be found, the plaintiffs may be able to overcome work product protection and gain access to the private investigator's memo. On the other hand, some *types* of work product are never supposed to be subject to discovery. As the Rule says, "opinions, theories, conclusions, and legal theories" are not to be discovered. So if the private investigator's memo contained the investigator's conclusion that the wreck was caused by faulty operation, that part of the memo should not be subject to discovery.

Enforcing the Discovery Provisions

Each discovery tool imposes a duty on the responding party (RP). For example, she must respond to interrogatories, requests to produce, and requests to admit within 30 days of their being served on her. Sometimes, RP does not respond at all. Sometimes, she responds to some of the individual questions or requests but not to others. Often, there is a good reason for this. She might find the questions or requests improper—for example, because they seek discovery of irrelevant or privileged or protected matter. In that case, RP should respond on time and answer the questions she can answer while objecting in appropriate detail to the ones to which she objects. Or, in the alternative, she might move for a protective order under Rule 26(c). This would be an order from the court that she not be required to respond on certain matters.

Let's say RP answers some interrogatories (or responds to some requests to produce) and objects to others. If the propounding party thinks the objections are bogus, she may make a "motion to compel" responses under Rule 37(a)(1). The court will then hear arguments and decide either to grant or deny the motion. If it grants the motion, the court will be agreeing with the propounding party that RP did not play by the rules—she should have answered these questions. But RP will be subject only to a minor sanction: an order compelling her to answer the questions (plus she will have to pay the costs and attorney's fees that the other side incurred in bringing the motion).

Suppose the court orders RP to answer the unanswered questions and RP refuses to do so. Bad mistake. Violating an order to compel opens RP to the significant sanctions listed in Rule

37(b)(2)(A), including contempt of court (because she violated a court order[2]).

Now let's consider a different fact pattern: suppose RP fails completely to respond to interrogatories, requests to produce, or to appear at her own properly-noticed deposition.[3] Rule 37(d)(3) addresses this situation. It incorporates the significant sanctions in Rule 37(b)(2)(A) (with one exception—here RP cannot be held in contempt, because she has not yet violated a court order).

C. Pretrial Dismissal and Default

All cases end in one of several ways. First, most disputes settle, which results in an agreement between the parties detailing who will do what for whom, followed by P's voluntary dismissal under Rule 41(a). Second, many cases are dismissed involuntarily. The Rule 12(b) defenses—which include lack of subject matter jurisdiction and lack of personal jurisdiction—are classic examples. Other bases for involuntary dismissal are found in Rule 41(b), which provides that a court may dismiss because of P's failure to prosecute the case or to abide by court orders or rules.

In some cases, D fails to respond within the time prescribed by the Rules. D runs the risk of default and, worse yet, default judgment. Default is a notation made by the clerk of court on the docket sheet for the case. The requirements for having default entered are found in Rule 55(a). Though the Rule allows the judge to enter default, usually the clerk of court does it. Once default is on the record, D cannot answer or bring a motion. She must seek

---

[2]   Remember that a medical examination under Rule 35 can only be taken if the court orders it. If a party fails to show up for an ordered exam, we might expect the sanctions to include contempt. After all, the party failing to attend is violating a court order. But Rule 37(b)(2)(A)(vii) does not permit a finding of contempt in the Rule 35 context.

[3]   Remember that a party who fails to deny a request for admission (either a single request or an entire set) is deemed to have admitted the matter asserted.

to have the default set aside under Rule 55(c). In federal court, default is not automatically entered. Instead, once D's time for response has lapsed, P must ask the clerk to enter the default.

The default stops D from trying to contest the case, but does not entitle P to recover anything. To recover money or other relief, P will need to get a default *judgment* under Rule 55(b). Rule 55(b)(1) permits the clerk of court to enter the judgment in very limited circumstances. More often, P will seek entry of default judgment by the judge. The default judgment—like any judgment—gives P the legal right to the remedy stated. It can be enforced like any other judgment. D may seek to have a default judgment set aside under Rule 60(b).

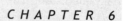

CHAPTER 6

The Litigation Process: Adjudication

A. Overview

At some point, cases that are not settled or dismissed (and in which the defendant (D) has not defaulted) become ripe for adjudication on the merits. That means we are going to find out what really happened—did D make a faulty product, was the plaintiff (P) really injured? Though trial by jury is the archetypal example of adjudication, we can adjudicate without trial, and we may have trial without a jury.

B. Adjudication Without Trial: Summary Judgment

It is important to appreciate the difference between dismissal for failure to state a claim under Rule 12(b)(6) (Chapter 5, § A) and summary judgment under Rule 56. Under Rule 12(b)(6), the court looked only to the face of the complaint. It did not look at evidence about what happened in the real world. The court assumed that P's factual allegations were true and asked whether they stated a plausible claim. If the answer was no, the case did not belong in the litigation stream.

With summary judgment, we are beyond that. The complaint states a claim, so if the facts alleged by P turn out to be true, and there is no applicable defense, P will win. Here, the court goes beyond the pleadings and may look at *evidence* about what really happened. But the purpose of considering evidence is *not to decide what happened*. The purpose is to determine *whether there is a dispute of fact about what happened*. There is only one reason to go to trial: to resolve disputes of fact. So if the evidence proffered by the parties in the motion for summary judgment shows that there is no genuine dispute on a material issue of fact, no trial is needed.

In sum, then: Rule 12(b)(6) weeded out cases that do not belong in litigation at all. Rule 56 weeds out cases that are properly in the litigation stream (we are in the right court, the complaint states a claim) but do not require a trial.

On a motion for summary judgment, the parties submit the evidence. "Evidence" means something under oath. Typically, parties use documents called affidavits or declarations, which are signed under penalty of perjury. Or the parties may proffer deposition testimony (because it is under oath) and answers to interrogatories (since they are under oath). In addition, the parties may rely on admissions made by the other party, either in response to a request for admission under Rule 35 or in the pleadings (such as when D fails to deny an allegation made by P).

Under Rule 56(a), the party moving for summary judgment must demonstrate (1) that there is no genuine dispute of material fact and (2) that she is entitled to judgment as a matter of law. The major focus is almost always on the first part. If the evidence shows that there is no dispute of fact, the only remaining question will be one of law. And the judge always determines matters of law.

Imagine it this way: the parties proffer evidence, which the court then puts into a basket. The judge then looks at all the evidence in the basket and asks one question: based on this evidence, is there a genuine dispute on a material issue of fact? If the answer is yes, summary judgment must be denied because the dispute of fact must be resolved at trial. If the answer is no, then the court may rule as a matter of law and enter summary judgment. The court is not required to grant summary judgment when the standard under Rule 56(a) is satisfied. It has discretion to deny summary judgment and require the parties go to trial.

> <u>Example</u>: P sues D, alleging in her complaint that P was a pedestrian, crossing the street with the green light, when D drove her car through a red light and ran into P. D files an answer in which she denies the material allegations. Now D moves for summary judgment, supported by affidavits of three eyewitnesses, all of whom state that they saw the event, that D had the green light, and that P jaywalked and jumped in front of D's car. In response, P submits no evidence. Instead, she relies on the allegation in her complaint that she had the green light and the D ran the red light.

Here, what is in the evidence basket? The affidavits from the three eyewitnesses, all of whom swear that D had the green light and that P jaywalked. Did P put any evidence in the evidence basket? No! Pleadings (like P's complaint) are *not evidence*. They are not signed under oath (in fact, they are not even signed by the parties—they are signed by the lawyer under Rule 11).[1] So based

---

[1] Occasionally, pleadings are executed under oath. These are called "verified" pleadings, and can be treated as affidavits on a motion for summary judgment. Verified pleadings are quite rare, applicable only in specialized types of cases. *See, e.g.,* FRCP 23.1 (verified complaint in shareholder derivative litigation).

on the evidence submitted, is there a genuine dispute as to a material fact? No—all the evidence tells the same story, and, as a matter of law, the court may enter summary judgment for D.

> Example: Same case, but assume D properly denied the allegations of P's complaint and then moved for summary judgment based upon affidavits from the three eyewitnesses (all saying that D had a green light). Suppose those three eyewitnesses were all wonderful, upstanding members of the community, known for the veracity and good faith. P opposes the motion by submitting deposition testimony from another eyewitness, who swears that D ran a red light. This eyewitness, however, has a reputation as a liar. The court will deny summary judgment. The evidence shows a dispute on a material fact, so the case must go to trial. The credibility of the witnesses is a question of fact to be resolved at trial. The goal in summary judgment is not to have the judge decide which version of the facts is right. The goal is to see whether there is a dispute of material fact, and thus a need to have a trial.

In *Scott v. Harris*, 550 U.S. 372 (2007), police pursued a speeding motorist and, while trying to force his vehicle into a spin, ran him off the road. The motorist sued the officers to recover for his personal injuries. The officers moved for summary judgment based upon a video taken from the police vehicle during the chase. They claimed that the driver had been acting in a way that endangered human life, which would excuse their actions. The Court approved summary judgment for the defendants because the video belied the plaintiff's version of the facts. Thus, the record included evidence that rendered the plaintiff's version of the facts unsupportable.

Many judges are reluctant to grant summary judgment. They worry about depriving the non-moving party of a trial. It is common for judges to say that in considering a motion for summary judgment, the court will view the facts in the light most favorable to the non-moving party. In 1986, the Court decided three cases, all sending the message that trial courts should not hesitate to use the tool in appropriate circumstances. In one of these cases, *Matsushita Electric Industrial Co. v. Zenith Radio Corp.*, 475 U.S. 574 (1986), the Court held that if two inferences are equally plausible on the facts—one supporting summary judgment and one not—it is proper for the court to adopt the one favoring summary judgment. In another, *Anderson v. Liberty Lobby*, 477 U.S. 242 (1986), the Court held that the non-moving party must produce more than a "scintilla" of evidence to support its version. Rather, it must produce enough evidence from which a reasonable jury could rule in its favor. If it fails to do so, summary judgment is proper.

The other 1986 case, *Celotex Corp. v. Catrett*, 477 U.S. 317 (1986), demonstrates that a defendant can prevail on a motion for summary judgment without submitting any evidence. The defendant, which had been sued for wrongful death allegedly caused by its product, made its motion by pointing out that the plaintiff had no evidence that the decedent had ever been exposed to the product it manufactured. Under *Celotex*, then, the party that does not have the burden of proof at trial may move for summary judgment by pointing out that the record is devoid of evidence that supports the other side's case. This point is now found in Rule 56(c)(1), which allows a motion because "a fact cannot be . . . supported." Once the motion is made, the burden shifts to the other party to put her cards on the table by submitting evidence that supports her position.

C. Adjudication at Trial

If the case is not resolved on summary judgment, we adjudicate the merits at trial. The purpose of trial is to resolve disputes of fact, so need a "fact finder." We also need to have someone instruct the fact finder on what the law requires—for example, to determine what facts (elements) the plaintiff must demonstrate to prove her claim. The judge always performs this latter function of determining what showing the law requires. The fact-finding function, however, may be performed by a jury or, if there is no jury, by the judge. When the judge acts as fact-finder, we have a "bench trial."

Jury Trial

Most countries do not have trial by jury, but in the United States it is nearly a sacred right. The jury—a group of laypeople, drawn at random from the community—is the voice of democracy in the judicial system. We repose great trust in the wisdom of the common person. The right to a jury is so fundamental that it is the subject of two provisions of the Bill of Rights. The Sixth Amendment guarantees trial by jury in criminal cases. We focus on the Seventh Amendment, which addresses jury trials in civil cases. The Seventh Amendment applies only to civil cases in federal court. It does not apply in state courts. Nonetheless, most states guarantee the right to jury in civil cases, usually along lines similar to those discussed here under the Seventh Amendment.

The Seventh Amendment consists of two provisions. One, our focus here, concerns the right to a jury in federal civil cases. The other, the "re-examination clause," provides that no fact determined by a jury may be re-examined by any court except on bases permitted by the common law. We will see that in § D.

The Seventh Amendment uses curious language in bestowing the right to jury trial. First, it does not "create" or "grant" a right to jury trial. Rather, it says that the right shall be "preserved." Second, it does not preserve the right in all cases, but only "[s]uits at common law." Because the right is "preserved," the Supreme Court has long held that we must consider whether P would have had a right to a jury in 1791. Why? Because that is when the Seventh Amendment was ratified. Moreover, the question is whether one would have had a jury right in 1791 "at common law"—and that means pursuant to the common law of England! So whether one has a right to trial by jury in federal civil cases in the twenty-first century depends upon whether one would have had the right in 1791 at common law in England.

In 1791 in England, there were two systems of civil justice— courts at common law and courts of equity. This bifurcation was followed in every state and in the federal courts in this country. Over time, most systems morphed to having one set of trial courts, but with a "law side" and an "equity side." These "sides" had different procedural rules and different terminology. In the federal courts, we finally abolished separate procedures and terminology for law and equity in 1938, with the adoption of the Federal Rules of Civil Procedure. Now, in federal court, there is only one type of case, the "civil action."

But the abolition of separate rules for law and equity cases in the federal (and most state) courts does not render the distinction between law and equity irrelevant. Indeed, it is still crucial. Among other things, as we see here, the right to jury trial under the Seventh Amendment depends on whether our case would have been "at common law" in England in 1791 (as opposed to "at equity" in England in 1791).

We need a bit of history. After William the Conqueror defeated the Britons (1066 and all that), he established various royal courts. To invoke the jurisdiction of these courts, P was required to plead the appropriate "writ." Over time, the royal courts expanded their jurisdiction but suffered from two significant problems. First, they became obsessed with technicality. If P chose one writ but the evidence at trial supported a different claim, P lost. Many plaintiffs were denied access to justice because they did not cross all the T's and dot all the I's on these and other arcane rules. Second, the royal courts were not creative about the remedies. They recognized one: "damages," which is money to compensate P for harm suffered. To this day, damages are the paradigmatic remedy "at law."[2] Damages are important, but sometimes damages will not make P whole.

> Example: D continually trespasses over P's land. P could sue for damages, which would compensate her for the harm caused by the past trespassing. Damages will not stop D, however, from trespassing in the future. D may continue doing so, merely paying damages for the privilege. P really wants an *injunction*: a court order telling D not to trespass. If D violates the court order, he can be jailed for contempt.

But the royal courts (generically the "common law courts") would not give a remedy other than damages. Plaintiffs left out in the cold because of the royal courts' obsession with technicalities or frustrated by the inability to obtain a remedy other than damages petitioned the Chancellor (who was a member of the King's Council) to "do equity." Over several centuries, this practice developed into a separate set of courts—the equity (or chancery) courts. These courts developed their own remedies. Equity courts issued injunctions, declaratory judgments,

---

[2]   Not every monetary recovery constitutes "damages." Recovery of money to disgorge D's unjust enrichment, for example, may be restitution, which is an equitable remedy.

rescission, ordered reformation of documents and "specific performance," which required a party to do something she agreed to do (like execute a deed). To this day, these are called "equitable" remedies.[3] In the common law courts, juries determined the facts, but in the equity courts, there was no right to a jury.

Now, back to today. Under the Seventh Amendment, we get a jury in a federal civil case if we would have had one at common law in England in 1791. To figure that out, the Supreme Court has imposed a two-part test. First, the judge must determine whether P's claim had an analog in the common law of 1791. This is a daunting question, because many claims we take for granted today (like strict liability and negligent infliction of emotional distress) were not recognized in 1791. Moreover, judges are not legal historians and do not feel comfortable making this assessment. Most courts take a half-hearted stab at it and find some ancient writ that would have come close to the present claim. The second inquiry is much more important: is the remedy legal or equitable? If what P wants is compensation for harm already done, she is entitled to a jury. If not, she is not entitled to a jury.

What about cases that involve some law and some equity? In the Example above, suppose P seeks (1) damages for past trespass and (2) an injunction against future trespass. Until the 1950s, federal courts took an all-or-nothing approach based upon what they thought was the main thrust of P's case. So if the judge thought the injunction was the most important part of P's case, there would be no jury on anything, because the injunction is an equitable remedy. Today, it's different. P is entitled to a jury on all factual issues underlying her law claim (the claim for damages)

---

[3]   And to this day, even in systems that have combined law and equity, a plaintiff cannot be given equitable relief until she shows that her legal remedy is inadequate—that is, as in the example above, that damages will not make her whole.

but not on facts that exclusively underlie the equity claim. So, in our example, the jury would decide the factual questions of whether D trespassed and, if so, what damages the trespass caused to P (because those facts underlie the damages claim). There would be no right to a jury, however, to determine whether P met the requirements for an injunction.

Even if the Seventh Amendment accords the right to have a jury determine the facts, the right is waivable. If any party makes a proper demand for jury trial under Rule 38(b), there will be a jury trial. If the parties fail to make such a proper demand, however, they will have waived the jury.

The judge instructs the jury on the requirements of the law. Though each party submits proposed jury instructions, the court is responsible for the instructions given. Instructions set the context in which the jury is to determine the facts. For example, the court will instruct that the plaintiff bears the burden of proof on elements of her claim, what the elements of that claim are, and what the burden of proof means. In most civil cases, the burden is to show facts by a "preponderance of the evidence," which means to establish to the jury's conclusion that the fact is more likely than not. Defendant has the burden to establish facts supporting any affirmative defenses. The judge usually reads jury instructions immediately before the jury is to deliberate.

The Difference Between Verdict and Judgment

The jury's decision is the "verdict." Often, the jury returns a "general verdict," which simply states that the jury finds for P or D. The court may, however, give the jury a special verdict form or a form with specific questions. For example, the verdict form might ask whether D owed a duty to P. If so, it might ask whether D breached that duty. If so, it might then ask whether the breach caused harm to P, etc.

The verdict should not be confused with the "judgment," which is always entered by the court. The judgment is the official announcement by the court of the resolution of adjudication. Whether a case is adjudicated by jury or bench trial or by motion for summary judgment, it ends in entry of a judgment. The judgment in a jury case reflects the finding of the jury (so the judgment is "based upon the verdict"). The judgment is a short document, the operative language of which is usually one sentence, such as "judgment is entered for the plaintiff in the sum of $150,000, plus costs."

D. Motions for JMOL, RJMOL, and New Trial

In criminal cases, D always has a right to "go to the jury"— that is, to have the jury decide her fate. This is true even if evidence of guilt is overwhelming—indeed, even if D admits she's guilty! And the jury in criminal cases always has the right to acquit the defendant. This "jury nullification" allows a body of citizens to stand up to the government and exonerate someone for any (or no) reason.

Civil cases are different. Even when which the Seventh Amendment applies, there is no absolute right to "go to the jury." The court plays a role in ensuring that there is sufficient evidence to warrant having the jury decide the facts. It does this through two motions: the motion for judgment as a matter of law (JMOL) under Rule 50(a) and the renewed motion for judgment as a matter of law (RJMOL) under Rule 50(b). These motions do the same thing, but come up at different times. JMOL is a motion made by a party *at trial*. RJMOL is a motion made by a party *after trial*, within 28 days after the court enters judgment.

The function of these motions is the same as a motion for summary judgment. That motion, discussed in § B, was brought *before trial*, based upon evidence proffered by the parties. It weeded out cases in which there was no genuine dispute on a material issue of fact and thus in which there was no need for trial. Now, for whatever reason (perhaps nobody moved for summary judgment), the case has gone to trial and we find that the evidence as presented *at trial* fails to justify having the jury consider the matter. Though neither Rule 50(a) nor 50(b) uses this phrase, courts enter JMOL or RJMOL because the evidence presented at trial showed that reasonable people could not disagree on the result. In other words, based upon what the parties showed at trial, there is no genuine dispute on a material issue of fact.

The motion for JMOL cannot be made until the non-moving party has presented her evidence at trial. At trial, P goes first, presenting her evidence through witness testimony and the introduction of evidence. P's witnesses may be cross-examined by D's lawyer. At some point, P "rests," meaning she has put on her evidence. At that point, D may move for JMOL, because P has been heard. (P could not move for JMOL at this point, because D has not presented her evidence yet.) If the court does not grant D's motion for JMOL (if she made one), then D puts on her evidence. Her witnesses are subject to cross-examination by P's lawyer. At some point, D "rests." Then, P may move for JMOL.

> Example: Assume that the relevant law requires P to demonstrate four elements to win on a claim: W X, Y, and Z. At trial, P puts on evidence that W, X, and Z happened. She presents no evidence that Y happened. D moves for JMOL. The court may grant it. Reasonable people could not disagree: because P failed to show that Y happened, and that is an element of her claim, no reasonable person could find for P. (Historically, was called a motion for "directed verdict," which is language

still used by most state courts and by many lawyers and judges in federal court.)

Suppose, however, that the court denies D's motion for JMOL. This happens sometimes because the judge is nervous about granting JMOL. After all, it takes the case out of the jury's hands. The judge may well assume that the jury will get the right answer and bring back a verdict for D. Most times, it will. But suppose it brings back a verdict for P. The court enters judgment on the basis of the verdict. This is where RJMOL can come into play. Within 28 days after entry of the judgment, D can move for RJMOL under Rule 50(b). On the facts of our example, it should be granted. Why? Because based upon the evidence presented at trial, reasonable people could only come to one conclusion: D should win because P has no evidentiary support for one element of her claim. In other words, the jury reached a conclusion reasonable people could not have reached. (Historically, this motion was called "judgment notwithstanding the verdict," which is quite descriptive; many state courts retain the older terminology.)

Notice how extraordinary JMOL and RJMOL are. With JMOL, we have gotten all the way to trial and one party lacks sufficient evidence to get to the jury. With RJMOL, the court takes victory away from one party and enters victory for the other party. Because these motions are so intrusive of the jury function, they are used with caution, The re-examination clause of the Seventh Amendment provides that a jury determination cannot be second-guessed except as permitted by common law. Because common law permitted what we now call RJMOL, it is allowed, but only if the party moving for RJMOL moved for JMOL at a proper time at trial. So in our example, if D had failed to move for JMOL after P had put on her evidence at trial, she would have waived the right to seek RJMOL.

These motions differ radically from the motion for new trial under Rule 59(a)(1). New trial, like the motion for RJMOL, must be made within 28 days after entry of judgment. But its function is different. If the court grants RJMOL, it takes the judgment away from one party and enters judgment for the other party. Either way, the case is over. If the court grants new trial, the court takes judgment away from the winner and says that the parties must re-try the case. It is a do-over. Maybe the same party will win, maybe the other party will win. So new trial is less drastic that RJMOL. Both take victory away from the verdict winner, but new trial does not declare a winner.

A court may order a new trial under Rule 59(a)(1)(A) for any reasons historically recognized at common law. The Rule does not catalogue such reasons, but they amount to this: the court may order new trial when it is convinced that something was so wrong with the first trial that it affected the outcome and the parties should try the case again. For example, maybe the judge made a mistake and put the burden of proof on the wrong party. Or maybe the jury went out to the scene of the accident and made an independent investigation, rather than basing its verdict on the evidence presented in court.

Whatever the basis for new trial is, the problem must have been "prejudicial." Trials are human endeavors, and like any human effort, there will be mistakes. We do not require perfection, and will not order a new trial just because something was not done perfectly. The error must have important enough—not merely "harmless error"—to make the judge conclude that justice requires a new trial. For example, to order new trial on the basis that the damages verdict was too low or too high, the court must find that the figure set by the jury "shocks the conscience."

Example: D, driving her car, hits P, who is riding a bicycle. P suffers a broken wrist and misses one week of work, suffered pain, and her bicycle (worth $200) was destroyed. The jury returns a verdict for P and sets damages at $300,000. The court concludes that the evidence of liability was clear but that the damages figure is shockingly high. It can order a new trial of the entire case. Or it can order a new trial on damages alone (since liability was clear).

New trials are expensive for the parties and the court. Sometimes courts will try to induce the parties to avoid going through a new trial. In this Example, the court could suggest remittitur, which says to P, essentially: "either you take a lower figure (say, $20,000), or I will order new trial." The implicit message is that P might not win anything at the new trial, so she should take the lesser figure and be happy. The court has no authority to set a new damages figure, so P is not required to accept. She can reject remittitur and take her chance with the new trial.

Let's try the flip side: suppose P shows that she suffered catastrophic injuries, but the jury returned a verdict of only $20,000. The court could order a new trial on all issues or (if liability was clearly established) on damages alone. It might be tempted to play hardball with D through something called additur. This would say to D, essentially: "either you pay a larger figure (say $500,000), or I will order a new trial." The implicit message is that at the new trial a jury may impose enormous liability on D. The problem is that additur is unconstitutional! It violates the Seventh Amendment, so cannot be used in federal court. Remember, though, the Seventh Amendment does not apply in state court, so state courts are free to use additur. Again, the court has no right to change the damages figure set by the jury. A party can always reject the suggestion made by the court and go through the new trial.

CHAPTER 7

The Litigation Process: Appellate Review

A. The Nature of Appellate Review

Most of what we study in Civil Procedure takes place in a trial court, like the federal district court. In Chapter 1, § B, we discussed the three-tiered model adopted in the federal (and many state) judicial systems. We speak in this chapter of appeals from the trial court to the intermediate court of appeals. There is no federal constitutional right to appeal in civil cases. Congress has provided a statutory right, however, to appeal final decisions of district courts to the United States Court of Appeals. Recall from Chapter 1, § B, that appellate courts do not re-try cases. There is no jury or fact-finding. Instead, they review the case "on the record," looking at the pleadings, motions, orders, judgment, and, if there is one, the trial transcript.

Appellate courts apply different standards to review various rulings of the trial court. The standards reflect different degrees of deference to the trial judge on the types of rulings. On matters of law, appellate review is "de novo," which means no deference is accorded the trial judge's interpretation. On findings of fact, though, the appeals court can reverse only if the trial court was "clearly erroneous." In other words, there is a presumption that the trial court reached the right decision on matters of fact. This presumption, which recognizes that the fact-finder was in a position to watch witnesses and to draw conclusions about veracity, is especially strong in jury cases. Finally, there is a range of decisions that are discretionary with the trial court, such as whether to allow an extension of time to answer, or what sanctions to impose for discovery abuse, or whether to allow amendment of pleadings. On these matters, the appellate court will reverse only if the trial court "abused its discretion." It will affirm so long as the trial decision was within the realm of reasonable decisions.

B.　The Final Judgment Rule

In the federal system, 28 U.S.C. § 1291 gives a right to appeal to the United States Court of Appeals only from "final decisions" by the federal district court. The appellant must file her notice of appeal in the trial court within 30 days of entry of the final judgment.

Though § 1291 speaks of final "decisions," the courts interpret it to require a final "judgment." A final judgment is one that completely concludes the consideration of the merits of the dispute. It is final if all that remains for the trial court is the ministerial housekeeping of assessing costs or attorney's fees. To determine whether a ruling is appealable under § 1291, ask: after making this ruling, does the trial judge have anything left to do on the merits of the case? If the answer is yes, the ruling is not an appealable final judgment.

> Example: P sues D for breach of contract. D files a counterclaim against P. The court enters summary judgment in favor of P on the counterclaim by D. D

cannot appeal that ruling under § 1291. Even though the ruling completely adjudicated the counterclaim, it did not resolve the entire case. Because P's claim against D is still pending, there is no final judgment yet.

Example: After two years of litigation and full trial, P wins a jury verdict and judgment of $500,000. The court then grants D's motion for new trial, which means P loses her judgment and must start over with a new trial. Can she appeal the grant of new trial under § 1291? Well, let's ask: after ordering new trial, does the trial court have anything left to do on the merits of the case. Yes—it must hold the new trial! Accordingly, the grant of new trial is not a final judgment.

Example: Same facts as the previous hypo, except the court denies D's motion for a new trial. Is that appealable? Yes, because after denying new trial, the trial court has nothing left to do on the merits of the case. D will file notice of appeal within 30 days of the denial of new trial.

The final judgment rule can be frustrating, because it prohibits review of many important rulings on which the trial judge may have made a mistake. Perhaps you think the court erred when it denied your motion to dismiss for lack of personal jurisdiction or when it permitted amendment of pleadings. Those are not final judgments, though, so you cannot appeal. You must be careful to make your objection to the rulings as they are made. Then, if you lose the final judgment, you may raise all these issues then.

Though frustrating, the final judgment rule makes sense. It avoids piecemeal appeals, which would delay trial-court resolution of the case. It also avoids unnecessary appeals, because the party that lost on various individual rulings might win the case on the merits. In that instance, its argument about error becomes moot.

C. Interlocutory Review

Because the final judgment rule can thwart appellate review of important issues, it is not absolute. There are several avenues to allow immediate review of "interlocutory" rulings (which are any rulings that are not final judgments).

Statutory Provisions

28 U.S.C. § 1292(a) expressly permits appeal of specific types of interlocutory orders. Most important is § 1292(a)(1), dealing with orders concerning injunctions. Thus an order granting or denying an injunction, though interlocutory, is appealable.

Section 1292(b) allows interlocutory review of certain orders, but requires that both the district court and court of appeals agree that the matter should be reviewed now. The district court must certify that its order (1) involves a "controlling question of law" (2) as to which "there is substantial ground for difference of opinion," and (3) that immediate appeal might facilitate termination of the litigation. The court of appeals must then agree to accept the appeal. This is a salutary provision because it allows the immediate appeal of a difficult question of law which might ultimately be decisive. The district judge who ruled on the matter might think it such a close question that immediate appellate review would be salutary.

Federal Rules Provisions

Rule 23(f) gives the court of appeals discretion to review orders granting or denying certification of a class action. Such an order is not final because it does not resolve the underlying dispute on the merits. But it is usually of critical importance. Granting certification will hasten settlement because D will not want to face aggregate liability. Denying certification will often sap the class representative's lawyer's initiative because all that remains is a single (often small) claim. Rule 23(f) allows review of the order without having to await final judgment.

Rule 54(b) allows the trial court to treat certain rulings as final judgments. It applies only in cases involving multiple parties or multiple claims. The district judge who enters an order completely resolving one of those claims (or resolving everything as to one of the parties) may enter "final judgment" as to that claim or party. If she also certifies that there is no just reason to delay appellate review, the order is appealable (the court of appeals has no authority to refuse to hear this appeal).

Rule 54(b) is best understood not as an exception to the final judgment rule, but as shifting the focus of that rule. Instead of asking whether a ruling determines the merits the entire dispute, here we ask whether the order determines the merits of a separate claim or as to a separate party in the case. Let's revisit the first Example we saw in § B. P sued D and D filed a counterclaim against P. The court entered summary judgment in favor of P on the counterclaim by D. D could not appeal under § 1291 because the order did not resolve the entire case. On the other hand, because the summary judgment did completely resolve the counterclaim, the district judge can (under Rule 54(b)) enter final judgment as to the counterclaim and certify that there is no just reason to delay appellate review.

Common Law

Courts of appeals have discretion to hear interlocutory matters under the "collateral order" doctrine. The leading case is *Cohen v. Beneficial Industrial Loan Co.*, 337 U.S. 541 (1949), which established these requirements: the issue appealed must be (1) legally significant, (2) unrelated ("collateral") to the merits of the underlying dispute, (3) determined finally (not subject to reconsideration) by the trial court, and (4) effectively unreviewable if the parties must wait until final judgment. The collateral order doctrine is rarely invoked successfully.

> Example: Under the Eleventh Amendment, states generally are immune from being sued in federal court. (Note that this is not simply immunity from liability, but immunity from being sued at all.) P, a contractor hired by the state highway department, sues the department for breach of contract. D moves to dismiss because it is an "arm of the state" and therefore entitled to Eleventh Amendment immunity from suit. The district court denies the motion. The issue may qualify for immediate appellate review because (1) the issue legally significant, (2) has nothing to do with the merits of the underlying dispute (whether there was a breach of contract), (3) has been decided finally, and (4) if it has to await final judgment, the department will be robbed of immunity from suit. The Eleventh Amendment protects states (and "arms" of states) from being sued in federal court at all. If the department must go through litigation in the meantime, it will be robbed of that right.

Extraordinary Writ

Occasionally, a litigant may ask an appellate court to enter an order (a writ) addressed directly to the lower court. Such a writ might command that court to do something (a writ of mandate or mandamus) or might command that the court not do something (a writ of prohibition). Technically, these are not appeals but are separate proceedings initiated in the appellate court. They are not available simply to police erroneous rulings by the lower court, but are limited to cases in which the lower court is basically abdicating a responsibility or acting beyond its jurisdiction. For example, if a district court proceeded with a case in which there was no federal subject matter jurisdiction, the court of appeals could issue a writ commanding the district court to dismiss the case.

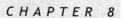

CHAPTER 8

Defining the Scope of Litigation: Joinder of Claims and Parties

To this point, we have taken a case all the way through the litigation stream: from selection of a forum to pleading and discovery to adjudication to judgment and through appellate review. But the suit was rather simple. We largely assumed that there was one plaintiff (P) suing one defendant (D). Now we are going back to see how a case might become more complex. The joinder provisions of the Federal Rules define the scope of litigation: how many parties and how many claims may be packaged into a single case?

Professors like the joinder material for several reasons. First, joinder provisions are mechanical, so they give straightforward material to test. You simply have to roll up the sleeves and learn some nuts-and-bolts rules.

Second, however, joinder raises an important policy clash. On the one hand, we value litigant autonomy, and feel that plaintiffs should be able to choose whether to join with other plaintiffs and how many defendants should be in the case. On the other hand, we value efficiency. Courts are public resources and we have a right to expect that they not be wasted. So there may be times when other parties, the court, and maybe even non-parties should be permitted to override P's preferences regarding case structure. Moreover, we are concerned that if the case becomes too complex, individual litigants will lose their sense of access to justice, of having their voice heard.

Third, joinder rules give the professor a chance to test *subject matter jurisdiction*. Remember that every single claim ever asserted in federal court—not just the original claim that gets the case into court, but every claim ever joined—must invoke federal subject matter jurisdiction. If it does not, it cannot be included in the case. It must be pursued in state court. Accordingly, every time you see a claim asserted in federal court, you should test to see if it invokes either diversity of citizenship or federal question jurisdiction. If so, the claim can be joined. If not, then we test to see if the claim invokes supplemental jurisdiction (Chapter 3, § D).

Remember: *every time a joinder rule permits the assertion of a claim in federal court, that claim must be assessed for federal subject matter jurisdiction.* Be relentlessly mechanical: First, find a joinder rule that allows the assertion of the claim. Second, assess subject matter jurisdiction over that claim. When assessing subject matter jurisdiction, be equally relentless: try diversity, try federal question and, if neither of those is met, try supplemental jurisdiction.

A. Permissive Party Joinder ("Proper Parties")

If one plaintiff wants to sue one defendant, no party joinder rule is implicated. She just does it and then we would see if the case invokes diversity of citizenship or federal question jurisdiction. But suppose P wants to sue multiple defendants. Or suppose multiple plaintiffs want to sue a single or multiple defendants. P (or plaintiffs) will use Rule 20(a). Rule 20(a)(1) permits multiple plaintiffs to join together if their claims (1) arise from the same transaction or occurrence (T/O) and (2) raise at least one common question. Rule 20(a)(2) permits joinder of multiple defendants in the same circumstances: if the claim against them (1) arises from the same T/O and (2) raises at least one common question.

Notice that Rule 20(a) *permits* joinder of multiple parties but does not require it. This is made clear by the provision that one "may" (as opposed to "must") join the parties and explains why this is called "permissive party joinder." There may be strategic reasons for not joining particular parties. For example, some plaintiffs prefer to sue alone, without joining other potential plaintiffs. That way, the thinking goes, the jury will focus entirely on her injuries, undistracted by another victim. Or perhaps a potential defendant is not subject to personal jurisdiction in the forum or perhaps joinder of some parties will make it impossible to invoke diversity of citizenship jurisdiction. Those who are joined under Rule 20(a) are called "proper" parties (as opposed to "necessary" parties, which we will see in § D).

> Example: A and B are passengers in a taxicab driven by Glen. The cab collides with a car driven by Glenda. A and B are injured. A and B may join as co-plaintiffs because their claims (1) arise from the same T/O and (2) raise at least one common question (who was at fault). For the same reason, they may sue both Glen and Glenda as co-defendants in a single case because the claims against those two (1) arise from the same T/O and (2) raise at least one common question.

Once P figures out how many plaintiffs and how many defendants she wants in the case, we then test to see if that case invokes federal subject matter jurisdiction. If it meets the requirements of diversity of citizenship or federal question jurisdiction, the case may go to federal court. If not, as structured, it must go to state court.

B. Claim Joinder by Plaintiff

Under Rule 18(a)(1), there are no limits on claim joinder. A claimant may assert "any" claims she has against D in a single case. The claims need not be related legally or factually. The rule is permissive, so P is not required to join multiple claims in one case. As a practical matter, the doctrine of claim preclusion will counsel P to join all transactionally related claims in one case to avoid having any subsequent case dismissed as precluded (we will study this in Chapter 9). Note that Rule 18(a)(1) applies not just to plaintiffs, but to any "claimant." As we will see, D may be a claimant—for instance, by asserting a counterclaim or crossclaim in the pending case. When she does, Rule 18(a)(1) then kicks into gear and allows her to join any and all other claims she may have against that defendant.

Remember, as with all joinder rules, Rule 18 is merely procedural. All claims joined will then have to be assessed for subject matter jurisdiction.

Example: P, a citizen of Missouri, sues D, a citizen of Arkansas. Under Rule 18(a)(1), P joins two claims against D: one for violation of her rights under federal employment law and one for damages of $100,000 for a totally unrelated state-law tort. Is this OK? Procedurally, it is fine because Rule 18(a)(1) permits joinder of any claims—even if they are factually unrelated. In terms of subject matter jurisdiction, Claim 1 invokes federal question jurisdiction because it is to enforce a federal right. Claim 2 invokes diversity of citizenship jurisdiction because a citizen of one state asserts it against a citizen of a different state and the amount in controversy for that claim exceeds $75,000. *Assess subject matter jurisdiction every claim separately!*

C. Claim Joinder by Defendant

In Chapter 5, § A, we studied various *defensive* maneuvers that a defendant can employ to try to avoid the imposition of liability on her. For instance, she can bring a motion to dismiss or can file an answer, in which she denies P's allegations and raises affirmative defenses. Here, we see D go on the offensive and file a *claim* against another party. There are two such claims: counterclaim the crossclaim. The terminology is confusingly similar, so be careful.

A *counterclaim* is asserted against an "opposing party." That means it is against somebody who has filed a claim against you. In most instances, then, it is by D against P. A *crossclaim*, in contrast, is against a "co-party." When will D have a co-party? When P used Rule 20(a)(which we saw in § A) to join multiple defendants.[1] When P joined D-1 and D-2 as defendants under Rule 20(a)(2), D-1 and D-2 became co-parties. If D-1 has a claim against D-2 in this case, it will be a crossclaim if anything.

Let's focus on the counterclaim. There are two types: compulsory under Rule 13(a)(1) and permissive under Rule 13(b). A *compulsory counterclaim* is one that arises from the same T/O as the underlying case. It is "compulsory" because it must be asserted in the present case and not in some separate proceeding. This result is implied by the provision that a party "must" (not

---

[1]   The case might have been structured with multiple plaintiffs under Rule 20(a)(1). So P-1 and P-2, as co-plaintiffs, might have sued D. P-1 and P-2 would be co-parties and a claim by one against the other would be a crossclaim. Crossclaims between co-plaintiffs, however, are pretty rare.

"may") assert the counterclaim. The compulsory counterclaim is unique: it is the *only* claim that must be asserted in the pending case. All other claims are permissive.

Example: A and B, each on a skiing vacation, collide on the slopes. A sues B to recover damages for her injuries. B answers and defends the case. Then B files a separate suit against A to recover damages for her injuries from the collision. B's case should be dismissed. When A sued B, they were opposing parties. B had a claim against A arising from the same T/O as A's claim against B. That made it a compulsory counterclaim, which "must" have been filed in the first case. Failure to do so means that B cannot sue on that claim. She has forfeited it. The purpose of the rule is to force transactionally related claims into a single case for efficient resolution.

A *permissive counterclaim* is one that is not compulsory—that is, one that does not arise from the same T/O as the underlying dispute. The defendant "may" (not "must") file the claim in the pending case. If she would prefer, however, she may assert the claim in a separate case.

A *crossclaim*, in Rule 13(g), is asserted against a co-party. There is another requirement: it *must* arise from the same T/O as the underlying dispute. Even though that is true, the crossclaim is *always* permissive; there is no such thing as a compulsory crossclaim. Rule 13(g) says the claim "may" (not "must") be filed in the pending case. So if D-1 would prefer, she can file a separate case against D-2 in which to resolve her transactionally related claim.

Example: P sues D-1 and D-2. D-1 has a claim against D-2 which has nothing to do with the underlying dispute by P against the two defendants. Can D-1 file her claim against D-2 in the pending case? No. It is not a crossclaim. Why? Because crossclaims must arise from the same T/O as the underlying case, and this claim does not. There is no joinder rule by which D-2 can file this claim in this case.

Suppose D-2 had two claims against D-1—one that arose from the same T/O as the underlying suit and one that did not. She could file the transactionally related claim as a crossclaim in the pending case. And once she filed crossclaim, she could use Rule 18(a)(1)(discussed in § B) to join the transactionally unrelated claim in the pending case.

So far, we have seen when a compulsory counterclaim, permissive counterclaim, and crossclaim are procedurally proper. Now remember: *every single claim in federal court must be assessed for subject matter jurisdiction.*

> <u>Example</u>: P, a citizen of South Carolina, sues two defendants, D-1 and D-2, both of whom are citizens of Tennessee for $500,000. The case arises from a boat collision. P was sailing her boat and D-1 was sailing the other boat, in which D-2 was a passenger. The case invokes diversity of citizenship jurisdiction. D-2 was injured in the crash. D-2 has a claim against D-1 (because the crash might have been her fault) and against P (because the crash might have been her fault). D-2's damages are $100,000. All claims arise under state negligence law. What claims may or should she file?

First, she should file a compulsory counterclaim against P. It is against an opposing party and arises from the same T/O as the underlying case. In fact, if D-2 does not file the claim in the pending case, she will forfeit it. The compulsory counterclaim invokes diversity of citizenship jurisdiction because it is asserted by a citizen of Tennessee against a citizen of South Carolina and exceeds $75,000.

Second, she may file a crossclaim against D-1, because D-1 is a co-party and the claim arises from the same T/O as the underlying case. But here is a problem: the crossclaim does not invoke diversity jurisdiction. It is asserted by a Tennessee citizen against a Tennessee citizen. (It also cannot invoke federal question because it is a state negligence claim.)

What do we do with a claim which cannot invoke diversity or federal question jurisdiction? We try supplemental jurisdiction. As discussed in Chapter 3, § D, this is a two-step analysis. First, does § 1367(a) grant jurisdiction? Yes if the claim shares a common nucleus of operative fact with the claim that got the case into federal court. This test (the *Gibbs* test) is always satisfied when claims arise from the same T/O as the underlying case. By definition every crossclaim arises from the same T/O as the underlying case. Second, does § 1367(b) take away supplemental jurisdiction over this claim? No. Though § 1367(b) applies in diversity cases (and this is a diversity case), it defeats supplemental jurisdiction only over claims by plaintiffs. This is a claim by a defendant, so § 1367(b) is irrelevant. Accordingly, D-2's crossclaim is supported by supplemental jurisdiction.

D. Necessary (Required) and "Indispensable" Parties

We saw in § A when P may use Rule 20(a) to join multiple plaintiffs or multiple defendants. We also saw that Rule 20(a) is permissive, and that P need not join all parties she could join. The present topic arises when P has not joined all the persons she could have joined. That means there is at least one "absentee" (non-party). Sometimes an absentee is so closely related to the pending case that he should be brought into the case.

Rule 19 permits a court to override P's party joinder by compelling an absentee to join the case. Though the Rule no longer uses this word, everybody calls such absentees "necessary" (the Rule says "required"). Rule 19 issues are easy to spot: we have a pending case, to which Absentee is not a party, and somebody (usually D) argues that Absentee should be brought into the case. The analysis proceeds in three steps.

First, is Absentee necessary? She will be necessary if she meets any of the three tests provided in Rule 19(a):

Test 1:   Absentee is necessary if, without her being joined, the court cannot accord complete relief among the parties (Rule 19(a)(1)).

Test 2:   Absentee is necessary if litigating without her may, as a practical matter, impair or impede some interest of Absentee's (Rule 19(a)(2)(i)).

Test 3:   Absentee is necessary if failure to join her might subject a party (that usually means D) to the risk of multiple or inconsistent obligations (Rule 19(a)(2)(ii)).

Though all three tests are of equal dignity under Rule 19, very few cases have ever discussed Test 1 meaningfully. Most cases involve a claim that Absentee should be joined under Test 2 or Test 3. With Test 2, we join Absentee to avoid having *Absentee herself* subjected to practical harm. With Test 3, we join Absentee to avoid subjecting *D* to the harm of multiple or inconsistent obligations. As a matter of policy, then, we have decided that P's prerogative to structure the case as must yield when her chosen structure threatens to harm Absentee or D in the ways specified.

Example: You own 100 shares of stock in Ace Corp. Along comes your evil cousin (EC), who claims that he paid for half the stock and that you and he agreed that you would hold the 100 shares in your joint names. EC sues Ace Corp., asking the court to declare that the stock is jointly owned by you and EC, your stock should be cancelled, and the 100 shares reissued in the joint name of you and EC. You are not a party to this case. Are you necessary?

Under Test 2, the answer is yes. Why? Because you have an interest in this matter (you say it's all your stock) and that interest may be impaired as a practical matter if the litigation goes forward without you. How? If EC wins the case, your stock will be cancelled. So you are necessary under Test 2, which is enough to justify bringing you into the case.

But there is another basis on which you are necessary. You also meet Test 3. That test focuses on potential harm to the defendant if Absentee is not joined. Suppose you are not made a party to this case. If EC wins, Ace Corp. will be subject to an order telling it to cancel your stock and reissue it with you and EC as joint owners. Then what will happen? Then you will sue Ace Corp. If you win that case, Ace Corp. will be subject to an order to keep the stock wholly in your name. Those two orders are inconsistent. Ace Corp. cannot satisfy one without violating the other. To avoid putting Ace Corp. in that situation, the court will find you necessary and try to bring you into the case.

The second step under Rule 19 is to ask whether the joinder of Absentee in the pending case is "feasible." Joinder will be feasible if the court has personal jurisdiction over Absentee and if joining Absentee will not make it impossible to maintain diversity jurisdiction. When the court considers your joinder, it decides whether you would come in a plaintiff or as a defendant. It does this by looking in a commonsense way at whether your interests align more with plaintiff or with defendant. On the facts of our case, you likely would be joined as a defendant, with Ace Corp. You and Ace Corp. agree that the status quo is fine. It is EC who is trying to change things in a way that hurts you.

Let's say the court decides that you should be joined as a defendant. Remember that joinder of parties is done for one reason: to allow the assertion of claims between those parties. Joining you as a defendant means that EC would file a claim against you. Remember too that every claim in federal court must be assessed for subject matter jurisdiction. So we would look to see whether EC's claim against you invoked diversity of citizenship or federal question jurisdiction. It seems unlikely that there would be a federal claim here, so diversity is more likely. If you are of diverse citizenship from EC and the claim against you exceeds $75,000, it will invoke diversity and your joinder is feasible.[2] If joinder of Absentee is feasible, the court orders joinder.

The third step in the process arises only if joinder of Absentee is *not feasible*. Again, it would not be feasible if the court cannot get personal jurisdiction over Absentee. It also would not be feasible if the claim by or against Absentee did not invoke subject matter jurisdiction. Then what happens? Under Rule 19(b), the court must do one of two things: either proceed in the litigation without Absentee or dismiss the entire pending case. It makes this decision based upon a balance of the four factors found in Rule 19(b). Courts have enormous discretion here, but usually the fourth factor—whether plaintiff has an adequate alternative forum if the case is dismissed—is the most important. Stated another way, courts are reluctant to dismiss unless there is some court (maybe a state court, where citizenship of the parties does

---

[2] When a claim is not supported by diversity or federal question, we try supplemental jurisdiction. Claims by or against necessary parties arise from the same fact patterns as the underlying dispute, so will invoke supplemental jurisdiction under § 1367(a). But § 1367(b) will create problems. If the case got into federal court originally under diversity jurisdiction, § 1367(b) thwarts supplemental jurisdiction over claims by plaintiffs against one joined under Rule 19 and over claims by Rule 19 plaintiffs. So claims by or against an absentee joined under Rule 19 cannot invoke supplemental jurisdiction (in a diversity case). All this is discussed in Chapter 3, § D.

not matter) in which everyone (including Absentee) can be joined in one case.

In common parlance, if the court decides to dismiss, we call Absentee "indispensable." In other words, "indispensable" is a label applied to a non-party who (1) is necessary but (2) whose joinder is not feasible and (3) in whose absence the court decides to dismiss. Rule 19 does not use the word, but lawyers and judges do. Rule 12(b)(7) is commonly known as the motion to dismiss for failure to join an indispensable party.

E. Impleader, or Third-Party Practice

When we addressed claim joinder by defendant in § C, we saw the counterclaim and the crossclaim. Here and in the next section we are going to learn about impleader and intervention. Here is a way to keep all these things straight. If a joinder rule starts with the letter C (counterclaim, crossclaim) it involves a claim between existing parties. Counterclaim is by a party against an opposing party. Crossclaim is by a party against a co-party. If the joinder rule starts with the letter I (impleader, intervention), a new party is being added to the case.

Rule 14(a) is the "impleader" rule (even though it says "third-party practice"). It permits D bring someone new (the "third-party defendant" (TPD)) into the case. D does this by asserting a claim against TPD. But not just any claim—D is suing TPD because TPD is liable to D *on the underlying claim by P against D.* This will almost always be a claim for indemnity or contribution.

Example: While P and D are driving their own cars, they collide and both are injured. P sues D. D's insurance company owes D indemnification on the claim by P against D. D can bring the insurance company into the case as a TPD by filing a third-party complaint against it.

Impleader fosters efficiency. Without it, D would have to litigate against P, and, if she lost, sue the insurance company in a second case to recover indemnification. With impleader, we get everything resolved in one case and D does not have to pay the judgment to P in the meantime. P's claim against D and D's right to indemnification are decided in one case.

Then we assess the impleader claim for subject matter jurisdiction.

> Example: P is a citizen of Florida. D is a citizen of Georgia. TPD is a citizen of Florida. All claims exceed $75,000. The claim by P against D invokes diversity of citizenship and gets the case into federal court. What about D's impleader claim against TPD? It also invokes diversity. D is a citizen of Georgia, TPD is a citizen of Florida, and the claim exceeds $75,000. Does it matter than TPD and P are citizens of the same state? Not at all. This claim is between D and TPD, so only their citizenships matter. P is not a party to this claim, so her citizenship is irrelevant.[3]

F. Intervention

Intervention is exactly what it sounds like: a non-party (Absentee) brings herself into a pending case. So, as with impleader and Rule 19, we are allowing someone (here the non-party herself) to override P's party structure of the case. Rule 24(b)(2) allows "permissive intervention" if Absentee's claim or defense and the pending case have at least one common question.

---

[3]   If P used Rule 14(a)(3) to assert a claim against TPD, it would not invoke diversity of citizenship, because each is a citizen of Florida. Would supplemental jurisdiction help? Assuming § 1367(a) were met, § 1367(b) would not allow supplemental jurisdiction. Why? This is a diversity case and that would be a claim by a plaintiff against someone (TPD) joined under Rule 14. Section 1367(b) prohibits supplemental jurisdiction over such claims. See Chapter 3, § D.

This is not much of a requirement—many assertions by non-parties may share a question with a pending case. The court has great discretion in deciding whether to allow permissive intervention. It will not do so if the result would be to delay or complicate the case unduly.

More interesting is "intervention of right" under Rule 24(a)(2). Here, Absentee has a right to come into the case in a rather limited situation—a situation we have already seen. Absentee must show that her interest may, as a practical matter, be harmed if she is not joined. (Though even then she has no right to intervene, according to the Rule, if her interest is adequately represented by somebody in the case—which is usually unlikely.) The operative language here is the same as in Rule 19(a)(2)(i), which we saw as Test 2 for necessary parties in § D. The concern is the same—if Absentee might be hurt by the pending litigation, then let's get her into the case. Rule 19 enables D to raise the issue. Rule 24 enables Absentee to take the bull by the horns and, as in The Price is Right, "come on down."

When Absentee intervenes, she chooses whether to join as a plaintiff or as a defendant. She makes this decision based upon which party is most closely aligned with her. You might ask: why would anyone choose to be a defendant? Consider the Example we saw in § D. You own 100 shares of Ace Corp. stock. Evil Cousin (EC) sues Ace Corp. to have your stock cancelled. Your interest may be harmed by this case. So you have a right to intervene (just as you were a necessary party in § D). Which side would you intervene on? Odds are you would choose the defendant's side. You have no disagreement with Ace Corp. It is EC you have trouble with. (If the court thinks Absentee intervened on the wrong side, it can "realign" her to the other side.)

An absentee intervenes either (1) to assert a claim or (2) to defend against a claim. Either way, there is a claim. And like all claims in federal court, we must assess it for subject matter jurisdiction. So do what we've done before: determine whether it invokes diversity of citizenship jurisdiction or federal question jurisdiction. If so, it may be asserted. If not, we try supplemental jurisdiction.[4]

G. The Class Action

Overview

A plaintiff brings a class action on behalf of herself and a group of persons who are "similarly situated." The plaintiff is called the "representative" ("Rep") and the group consists of class members. Technically, only Rep (or Reps, if there is more than one) is a party. Class members are not parties. Nonetheless, if we do it right, class members will be bound by the judgment. Ordinarily, one cannot be bound by a judgment unless she is joined as a party. As we will see in detail in Chapter 9, however, non-parties can be bound if their interests are adequately represented in litigation. Thus, class members are bound if Rep provides adequate representation of their interests. The class suit brings obvious economies of scale: instead of litigating in 1000 separate suits whether a product is defective, we can bind all 1000 claimants to one result—they either sink or swim together.

Prerequisites

Rep commences the class action by filing a complaint indicating that the case is brought on behalf of a class. At this point, however, it is only a "putative" class. It is not "officially" a

---

[4]   Claims by or against those who intervene of right will satisfy § 1367(a), because they involve the same facts as the underlying case. But § 1367(b) will be a problem, at least in diversity cases. That section (which applies only in diversity cases) prohibits supplemental jurisdiction over claims by plaintiffs against parties joined under Rule 24 and by claims by parties seeking to intervene as plaintiffs under Rule 24. See Chapter 3, § D.

class action until the court "certifies" it as such. To have a class certified, Rep must first satisfy *all* requirements of Rule 23(a). The four requirements are not hermetically sealed; factors relevant to one are often relevant to others.

First, the group must be so numerous that joinder is impracticable. This means that if we were left to the regular joinder rules (like Rule 20, discussed in § A), the case would not be manageable. There is no magic number, and the court will consider other factors, such as whether class members reside in the same place, which might make Rule 20 joinder easier to pursue.

Second, the claims of class members must have some commonality. It is not enough to say something like "they all want to win" or "they were all ripped off." The Supreme Court made clear in *Wal-Mart Stores, Inc. v. Dukes,* 131 S.Ct. 2541 (2011) that the issue is less about common questions than common *answers.* Rep must demonstrate that group resolution of issues will determine the cause of every class member.

Third, Rep's claim must be typical of those of the class members. Rep must suffer the same sort of harm as the class members.

Fourth, the representative must "fairly and adequately" represent the group. Without adequate representation, a judgment cannot bind class members. Rule 23(g) requires that the lawyer *also* adequately and fairly represent the group.

There is an implicit fifth requirement in Rule 23(a): that there be a class at all. It is important that Rep convince the court that this case will be manageable. Suing on behalf of some amorphous group that can never be identified—like "the downtrodden"—is a waste of time. The court must be convinced that there is a group out there for whom relief can be ordered (if they win) and who will be bound by the judgment (if they lose).

Types of Class Action

In addition to demonstrating satisfaction of Rule 23(a), Rep must show that the case meets the requirements of one of the types of class action permitted under Rule 23(b). Rule 23(b)(1) classes are quite rare in the real world. The 23(b)(2) is more likely—it is appropriate when D has treated the class alike and the remedy sought is an injunction or declaratory judgment. For example, a group of employees might claim that their employer has denied them promotions because of their age or sex or race. In *Wal-Mart* (2011), the Court made clear that the 23(b)(2) class generally may not be used to seek recovery for compensatory monetary relief (damages). The remedial focus must be injunctive or declaratory.

For exam purposes, Rule 23(b)(3) is by far the most likely. This is often called the "damages" class action because the group usually seeks compensatory monetary relief. For certification, Rep must show: (1) that common questions *predominate* over individual questions and (2) that the class action is the superior way to handle this dispute. For that first requirement, it is not enough just that the class members' claims present common questions—those common questions must *predominate* over individual questions.

> Example: A bus goes off the road and 80 passengers are injured. Everyone's damages will present individual questions because everyone is hurt in a unique way. But the common questions in the case—whether the driver was negligent or the bus defective or the driver of another vehicle caused the wreck—may predominate. So it may be proper to certify this class under Rule 23(b)(3)

to litigate *en masse* the question of liability, while leaving the litigation of damages to individual cases.

The Rule 23(b)(3) requirement that the class action be superior to other methods of litigating requires the court to compare the manageability of a class action to other options. The court will not take on the burdens of overseeing a class suit if the dispute could be more conveniently handled in another way.

Why is the 23(b)(3) most likely on the exam? Because there is more the professor can ask about. In the 23(b)(3) class *only*, the class members (after the class is certified) are entitled to notice telling them that they are members of a class, that they have a right to opt out of the class. Moreover, in this type of class *only*, the class members have a right to opt out. They can remove themselves from the class, in which case they will not be bound by the judgment. Opting out frees the class member to pursue her claim individually in a separate case. No notice or opt-out is required in the 23(b)(1) or 23(b)(2) classes.

Settlement

If the court certifies any type of class action, D has a huge incentive to settle. No defendant wants to roll the dice for aggregate liability based on the outcome of one case. So almost all certified classes settle. Unlike non-class cases, however, here the parties cannot simply reach their own binding agreement. Under Rule 23(e), the court must approve any settlement or dismissal. The court is in a fiduciary position to ensure that the proposed settlement is a "sweetheart" deal that lines the pockets of Rep's lawyer, lets D off the hook lightly, and leaves class members with no real remedy.

Subject Matter Jurisdiction

Rep may assert claims arising under federal law, which will invoke federal question jurisdiction. The more interesting proposition is how a class may invoke diversity of citizenship jurisdiction. Long ago, the Court held that, for citizenship purposes, we look only to the citizenship of the representatives. The class members do not matter. As long as the representative is of diverse citizenship from all defendants, we are OK. Oddly, the Court took the opposite tack, however, when it came to amount in controversy. In *Zahn v. International Paper Co.*, 414 U.S. 291 (1973), it held that each class members' claim must exceed $75,000.

Now, however, there is a way around *Zahn*. Suppose Rep (a citizen of Texas) brings a class action against D (a citizen of Louisiana). Rep's claim exceeds $75,000, but the other class members' claims are for less than that. Under *Zahn*, this will not work, because every member's claim must meet the amount in controversy requirement. In *Exxon Mobil Corporation v. Allapattah Services, Inc.*, 545 U.S. 546 (2005), the Court held that Rep's claim invoked diversity of citizenship jurisdiction (which got the case into federal court) and that the class members' claims invoked supplemental jurisdiction. (We covered supplemental jurisdiction in Chapter 5, § D.) Under § 1367(a), the class members' claims invoke supplemental jurisdiction because they share a common nucleus of operative fact with Rep's claim. And § 1367(b) does not take away that grant. Though § 1367(b) applies in diversity cases (like this one), it prohibits jurisdiction only over certain claims by plaintiffs. The list of prohibited claims does not include claims asserted under Rule 23. So supplemental jurisdiction gets the class members' claims into federal court—effectively overruling *Zahn*.

CHAPTER 9

The Preclusion Doctrines

A. Overview and Terminology

Do not let the terminology scare you. Whether your casebook calls this material "the doctrine of prior adjudication" or "claim and issue preclusion" or "res judicata," this material is about one thing: does the judgment entered in a case preclude the parties from litigating anything in a second case? For simplicity, we will refer to "Case 1" and "Case 2." (We do not care about the order in which the cases were filed; we care about the order in which they go to judgment.) Case 1 is over. Judgment has been entered. Now Case 2 is pending. There are two ways in which the judgment from Case 1 might stop the parties from litigating in Case 2: claim preclusion (or "res judicata") or issue preclusion (or "collateral estoppel").

Claim preclusion establishes that a claimant can only sue a defendant (D) once to vindicate a "claim" (or "cause of action"). You get one lawsuit per claim. So you must be careful to seek all rights to relief that are encompassed in that one claim in one case. If you do not—if you sue D twice on the same claim—claim preclusion will result in dismissal of Case 2. Claim preclusion makes sense: allowing a second suit on the same claim would waste judicial resources and harass D.

Issue preclusion is narrower. It precludes *re-litigation* of a particular issue that was actually litigated and decided in Case 1. It narrows the scope of Case 2 by deeming established in Case 2 an issue the parties litigated in Case 1. Let's say that in Case 1 the parties litigated several issues, one of which was whether Driver was negligent. Assume that that same issue is relevant in Case 2. If issue preclusion is applied, that issue will not be litigated again. Driver will be deemed negligent in Case 2. Assuming the parties had a full chance to litigate Driver's negligence in Case 1, it would be inefficient to re-litigate the question. It would also open the door to inconsistent findings of fact—in one case that Driver was negligent and in one that she was not. Such inconsistency can erode public confidence in the administration of justice.

If claim preclusion applies, Case 2 will be dismissed. If issue preclusion applies, Case 2 may proceed, but streamlined by the fact that previously determined issues of fact will be deemed established for purposes of Case 2.

B. Claim Preclusion

Claim preclusion applies if three things are true: (1) Case 1 ended in a valid, final judgment on the merits, (2) Case 1 and Case 2 are brought by the same claimant against the same defendant, and (3) the claimant asserted the same claim in Case 1 and in Case 2.

Valid, Final Judgment on the Merits

Only a valid, final judgment on the merits will have claim or issue preclusion effect. A valid judgment is one entered by a court that had personal jurisdiction and subject matter jurisdiction. A final judgment is one that wrapped up the merits of the entire dispute (basically the same as is required for appeal under the final judgment rule, Chapter 7, § B).

What, then, is a judgment "on the merits?" The phrase makes it sound as though the case went to trial. Certainly, a judgment resulting from a trial is on the merits. But summary judgment, though not resulting from a trial, is also a judgment on the merits. In fact, virtually any judgment in favor of a claimant will be deemed on the merits. For example, a default judgment is treated as on the merits because the default established the validity of the claim. A tougher case is presented by judgments against a claimant. Rule 41(b) provides that any involuntary dismissal *except those based upon jurisdiction, venue, or failure to join an absentee under Rule 19* "operates as an adjudication on the merits." Thus, dismissal for discovery abuse or for failure to comply with a rule or court order will have a preclusive effect, even though the merits of the case were not adjudicated (at trial or through summary judgment). So, in practice, "on the merits" does not require that the parties actually litigated anything in Case 1.

On the other hand, as Rule 41(b) makes clear, dismissals based upon lack of jurisdiction (personal or subject matter) or on improper venue or because of the failure to join an "indispensable" absentee under Rule 19 will not result in claim (or issue) preclusion. Some jurisdictions add to this list. For instance, in some states, a dismissal under the statute of limitations is not preclusive.

Same Claimant Versus Same Defendant in Both Cases

Claim preclusion prohibits a claimant from asserting the same claim twice. So it cannot apply unless the same litigant is asserting a claim against the same defendant in two cases. So do not fall for this head fake:

> Example: A and B, each driving her own car, collide and suffer personal injury and property damage. In Case 1, A sues B regarding the wreck. Judgment is entered. In Case 2, B sues A regarding the wreck. There is no role for claim preclusion here. While it is true that Case 1 and Case 2 involved the same parties, they did not feature the same claimant suing the same defendant. B was not a claimant in Case 1, so cannot be guilty of asserting the same claim twice. (In most jurisdictions, however, Case 2 would be dismissed. Why? Because of the compulsory counterclaim rule (Chapter 8, § C). When A sued B, B's claim against A arose from the same transaction or occurrence as A's claim and thus should have been filed in Case 1. But claim preclusion is wholly irrelevant.)

Notice that both cases must be brought by the same "claimant." Though all plaintiffs are claimants, not all claimants are plaintiffs. A defendant can be a claimant, for example, by asserting a counterclaim.

> Example: Same facts as above. In Case 1, A sues B regarding the wreck. B files a compulsory counterclaim against A. The case goes to judgment. In Case 2, B sues A again regarding the wreck. Case 2 might be dismissed under claim preclusion. Why? B has sued the same defending party (A) in Case 1 and Case 2. The fact that B

was a defendant in Case 1 does not matter. She was also a claimant, as she is in Case 2.

Claimant Asserted the Same Claim in Both Cases

A claimant is only in trouble under claim preclusion if she asserts the same claim twice. Jurisdictions can adopt different definitions of what constitutes a "claim." The trend is toward a broader definition. The result of a broader definition is to force the claimant to "pack" more elements of relief into a single case. This, in turn, fosters efficiency, which is a major goal of modern procedure.

An older definition (still used in a few states, including California) is that there are separate claims for each right invaded. This "primary rights" test focuses on the number of harms suffered by the claimant. A more modern approach—the "single wrongful act" test—provides that a claim consists of all harms suffered as a result of one wrongful act by the defendant. Still a more modern approach, embraced by the Restatement (Second) of Judgments, is that the claim consists of all rights to relief arising from a transaction or series of related transactions. Let's see the definitions in action.

> Example: D drives her car recklessly and rams into a car owned and driven by P. P suffers personal injuries and her car is destroyed. In Case 1, P sues D to recover for her personal injuries. The court enters a valid, final judgment on the merits. Now P sues D to recover for the damage to her car. Should Case 2 be dismissed under claim preclusion?

If the applicable law is the primary rights test, the answer is no. P has two claims, because D violated two separate rights: the right to bodily sanctity and the right to have one's property free from harm. So P is not asserting the same claim in Case 2 as she did in Case 1. The primary rights test is criticized as fostering inefficiency. After all, why should the courts be clogged with two cases about one real-world event?

If the applicable law is the "single wrongful act" test, Case 2 may be dismissed. P has only one claim because D was guilty of one bad act: she drove her car recklessly once and caused one collision. Because P is suing twice on the same claim, and because the other requirements are met, Case 2 may be dismissed under claim preclusion. And if the applicable law is the Restatement (Second), the answer is also yes. There has only been one transaction here, so there is only one claim. Note the effect of claim preclusion: it means that P will never get a day in court on her property damage claim. But we cannot feel sorry for P. After all, she could have (and, under these definitions of claim, should have) sought relief for the property damage in Case 1.

The single wrongful act and Restatement (Second) tests often lead to the same result, as here. We can imagine a case, though, where they would not. Suppose after the collision, D jumped out of her car and screamed threats at D, which caused D to fear physical harm. In a single wrongful act jurisdiction, this would constitute two claims because there were two wrongful acts: reckless driving and the intentional tort of battery. Under the Restatement (Second), however, there is likely only one claim because everything arose from a transaction or series of related transactions.

C. Issue Preclusion

Issue preclusion requires assessment of five things: (1) Case 1 ended in a valid, final judgment on the merits, (2) an issue in Case 2 was litigated and determined in Case 1, (3) that issue was essential to the judgment in Case 1, (4) *against whom* preclusion is asserted in Case 2, and (5) *by whom* preclusion is asserted in Case

2. The first factor is the same as in claim preclusion, which we discussed in the preceding section. So we need to address the remaining four.

Same Issue Litigated and Determined in Case 1

We saw above that claim preclusion may apply even if the parties did not litigate anything in Case 1. Issue preclusion is different. The issue on which a party seeks issue preclusion in Case 2 must have been litigated and determined in Case 1. Sometimes this requires the court in Case 2 to review the trial transcript from Case 1 to determine what issues were actually decided. For instance, a party may have presented facts supporting alternative theories of liability or defense. Issue preclusion applies only to those on which the judgment was actually based.

That Issue Was Essential to the Judgment in Case 1

It is not enough that the issue was litigated and decided in Case 1. It must also have been essential to the judgment. Sometimes, fact-finders make determinations on issues that turn out to be extraneous to the judgment. Issue preclusion does not apply to those extraneous matters, but attaches only to those issues on which the outcome in Case 1 depended.

> Example: P sues D for negligence and D asserts the defense of contributory negligence. The case is tried before a jury, which returns a special verdict saying that both P and D were negligent. The court enters judgment in favor of D. In a later case, the finding that P was negligent is entitled to issue preclusive effect but the finding that D was negligent is not. In a jurisdiction adopting contributory negligence, once P was found negligent, there can only be one judgment: P loses. It

does not matter whether D was negligent. So the finding that D was negligent was not essential to the Case 1 judgment in favor of D.

Due Process: Against Whom Issue Preclusion May Be Asserted

Due process forbids binding someone to a judgment unless she was properly joined as a "party" in the case (and brought within the jurisdiction of the court by proper notice). So as a matter of federal constitutional law, issue preclusion may only be used against someone who was a "party" in Case 1. The word party is in quotation marks because the courts have long recognized that *some non-parties may be bound by a judgment if their relationship with a party was so close that they may be considered parties.* Historically, such close relationships are gathered under the term "privity." Stated more accurately, then, issue preclusion may only be asserted against one who was a party or in privity with a party to Case 1.

The leading case is *Taylor v. Sturgell*, 553 U.S. 880 (2008), in which the Court catalogued six scenarios in which "nonparty preclusion" may be justified. All six are narrow. The Court made clear that these six scenarios do not exhaust all possibilities for binding a non-party to a judgment. Thus, due process would permit non-party preclusion more broadly than these six situations. Nonetheless, these are the most likely to be encountered.

One, a nonparty can agree to be bound by a judgment. Two, a legal relationship permits the conclusion that the party litigated on behalf of the nonparty. An example is successors-in-interest to land. Suppose a landowner sues his neighbor to assert an easement across the neighbor's land. The court rules for the neighbor and enters judgment. Now the landowner sells the property to you.

You are bound the previous judgment because of the substantive relationship of successor-in-interest (which you will study in Property). Three, the nonparty was adequately represented in Case 1 by a party, such as in a certified class action. Four, the nonparty controlled the litigation in Case 1, for example, by funding the case, hiring the lawyer, and making strategic decisions. Five, Case 1 was litigated by a party who was acting as agent of the nonparty. And six, some special statutory schemes expressly prohibit successive litigation. For instance, a legislature may provide that suit brought to enforce some public right may bind all members of the public.

> Example: A passenger plane operated by Airline Co. crashed, injuring 40 passengers. In Case 1, Passenger 1 sued Airline Co. At trial, the jury found that the crash was not the fault of Airline and the court entered judgment for Airline. In Case 2, Passenger 2 sues Airline about the same crash. Airline wants to assert issue preclusion as to the finding from Case 1 that it was not at fault. Airline cannot do so. Even though the issue was litigated and determined and was essential to the judgment in Case 1, Passenger 2 was not a party to Case 1. Neither did she fall within any of the six scenarios justifying nonparty preclusion. Due process prohibits the use of issue preclusion against Passenger 2, who is thus free to litigate the question of whether Airline was at fault.

Mutuality: By Whom Issue Preclusion May Be Asserted

We just saw that due process governs the question of "against whom" issue preclusion may be used. But due process is irrelevant to the topic of "by whom" it may be asserted. Rather, we must address "mutuality." This ancient concept provides that only someone who was a party to Case 1 should be able to assert preclusion in Case 2. Again, mutuality is not rooted in due process, so courts are free to reject it. Many courts have done so to permit "nonmutual" issue preclusion, at least in some circumstances.

One circumstance is "nonmutual defensive" issue preclusion (NDIP). Nonmutual means that the party using issue preclusion in Case 2 was not a party to Case 1. Defensive means she is a defendant in Case 2. Many (probably most) jurisdictions allow NDIP so long as the party against whom it is used had a full and fair opportunity to litigate in Case 1.

An example is *Blonder-Tongue Laboratories, Inc. v. University of Illinois Foundation* (1971). There, P held a patent on an invention. In Case 1, P sued D-1 for patent infringement. D-1 claimed that there was no infringement because P's patent was invalid. The court agreed and entered judgment for D-1. In Case 2, P sued D-2 for patent infringement. D-2 wanted to assert issue preclusion on the question that P's patent was invalid. That issue was litigated and determined and was essential to the judgment in Case 1. Moreover, there was no due process problem, because preclusion was being used against P, who was a party to Case 1. The problem was mutuality—preclusion was used by D-2, who was not a party to Case 1. The Court permitted NDIP, so long as P had had a full and fair chance to litigate the matters in Case 1 (which it had).

NDIP is a good idea. If it were not available, P could sue defendant after defendant and re-litigate the question of whether its patent was valid. It would not be bound by its loss in Case 1. This re-litigation would waste judicial resources and open the door to inconsistent results, which would erode public confidence in the judicial system. So long as P had a full chance to litigate in Case 1, she has had her day in court on that issue and ought to be bound by it.

The second circumstance is "nonmutual offensive" issue preclusion (NOIP). As always, nonmutual means that preclusion is being asserted by someone who was not a party to Case 1. Offensive means she is a claimant in Case 2. And again, the traditional view of mutuality would not allow this. Slowly, some jurisdictions (but probably not a majority) have permitted NOIP, but have recognized that we need to be careful about it. NOIP makes us nervous in ways NDIP did not.

Return to the airline crash case in which 40 passengers were injured. Suppose, as we saw above, Airline wins Case 1, based on a finding that it was not negligent. When Passenger 2 sues Airline, due process prohibits Airline from asserting issue preclusion (because Passenger 2 was not a party to Case 1). So if Airline is going to avoid liability, it must win all 40 cases. It can never use a victory against a new plaintiff.

Compare to this the situation in which a plaintiff wins Case 1. Then, if we allow NOIP, the others can that plaintiff's victory it in their own cases against Airline.

> Example: In Case 1, Passenger 1 wins, based upon a finding that Airline was negligent and caused Passenger 1's injuries. In Cases 2 through 40, NOIP would allow Passengers 2 through 40 to use the finding from Case 1 that Airline was negligent. Airline thus faces liability in 40 cases if it loses one. It can escape liability, however, only by winning all 40 cases.

We are nervous about NOIP because it reposes so much confidence in one victory for the plaintiffs. We are also nervous because it creates a disincentive to have efficient joinder in Case 1. When Passenger 1 sues Airline, the other 39 passengers will have no incentive to join in that case as co-plaintiffs. Instead, they will wait in the wings (so to speak) because they cannot be hurt by the judgment in Case 1. If Airline wins, it does not bind them (because of due process). But if Passenger 1 wins, NOIP will allow them to take advantage of that victory in their cases.

The Supreme Court recognized these concerns in *Parklane Hosiery Co. v. Shore*, 439 U.S. 322 (1979), and embraced NOIP only if it would be fair in light of all circumstances. It would not be fair, for instance, if the party in Case 2 who is asserting NOIP could have joined easily in Case 1. The Court was somewhat cryptic about what that means, but the idea seems clear: if you could have joined in Case 1 (perhaps through intervention), and you refused to do so, the court should not let you take advantage of the finding from Case 1. NOIP also would not be fair if there were inconsistent results on the record. For example, if Airline won some cases and then lost one, it would be unfair to let the later-suing passengers take advantage of the one victory. The fact that Airline won the other cases makes the passenger's victory look like a fluke. NOIP would also be unfair if the party against whom it is used did not have a full and fair opportunity to litigate in Case 1. Related to this is the idea that that party could not foresee multiple litigation—could not see, in other words, that a loss in Case 1 might haunt her in subsequent cases by other plaintiffs. In the Airline hypo, of course, it was plainly foreseeable that Airline would get sued by all 40 passengers.

CHAPTER 10

Erie

A. *Swift* and *Erie*

Many people consider "the Erie doctrine," which takes its name from *Erie Railroad Co. v. Tompkins,* 304 U.S. 64 (1938), the most difficult topic in Civil Procedure. The Supreme Court has not provided consistent guidance, which means that *Erie*—perhaps more than any other topic in Civil Procedure—is subject to varying interpretation by courts and professors. Be on the lookout for your professor's theory of *Erie*. It may make your life easier by providing a specific approach on your exam.

Erie issues are usually easy to spot. We are in federal court, almost always in a diversity of citizenship case, and the judge must decide some issue. The question is always the same: in deciding that issue, must the federal judge follow state law, or is she free to ignore state law? Why does *Erie* come up almost exclusively in diversity cases? Under the supremacy clause of the Constitution, when federal law applies, it trumps state law (assuming the federal law is valid). In federal question cases, federal law creates the claim and governs the substance of the dispute, so usually there is no role for state law. In diversity cases, however, the plaintiff (P) is suing on a state-law claim. So there is room for state law.

The Rules of Decision Act (RDA), 28 U.S.C. § 1652, provides (in circuitous language) that federal courts are to apply state "laws" except when federal laws apply. In *Swift v. Tyson*, 41 U.S. 1 (1842), the Supreme Court held that "laws" did not include "general common law." Common law means judge-made law, to be contrasted with legislation. "General" common law refers to the basic rules of contracts, torts, and property that govern our daily lives. Under *Swift*, federal judges in diversity cases could ignore state-court general common law and were free to make up what they thought was the best version of the law of contracts, torts, and property. Their version would apply in the cases they decided, but would not bind state courts. This led to significant trouble:

> Example: New York courts held that discharge of a debt
> did not constitute "consideration" for a contract.
> Federal courts in New York concluded that this was a
> silly view, and held—in diversity cases—that discharge of
> a debt did constitute consideration for a contract.

Those are the facts of *Swift*. The result was untenable because, for citizens of New York, the law meant one thing in state court and something entirely different in federal court. *Swift* was a doctrine of arrogance; it said that federal judges were the smartest kids in the room and had the right to divine what was the best, true common law. The implication was that the state courts should watch and learn from the masters in the federal courts.

Somehow, *Swift* was on the books for 96 years—until the Court overruled it in *Erie*. In *Erie*, the Court held that the regime ⸀ *Swift* violated the RDA. It could have based the holding entirely ⸀utory grounds by saying that "laws" in the RDA includes ⸀mon law. The Court went beyond this, however, and held—get this—that *Swift* was unconstitutional! Though it did not specify which part of the Constitution was violated, everybody agrees it was the Tenth Amendment. That clause provides that the states retain powers that are not expressly ceded (by the states and the people) to the federal government.

Because nothing in the Constitution gives the federal courts a power to declare the general common law, they have no such power. *Indeed, there is no such thing as general federal common law.* To the extent that common law governs daily life, the only kind is state-created. *Erie* is one of the most important cases in history. It admits that what the federal courts had done for 96 years was an unconstitutional usurpation of state power.

So on matters of general common law—including the basics of contracts, torts, and property—federal courts in diversity cases *must* follow state law. The federal bench has no power to make up its own law on those points in diversity cases.[1] Concurring in *Erie*, Justice Reed introduced labels that have stuck ever since: federal courts, he said, must apply "substantive" state law but should remain free to follow their own "procedural" law. The distinction was irrelevant in *Erie* because the question was whether the federal court was required to follow state law concerning the elements of the alleged tort. Nothing is more "substantive" than the elements of a claim or defense.

The labels "substantive" and "procedural" are not very helpful, because a lot of things (like statutes of limitations and burdens of proof) can be characterized as either. So "substance versus procedure" cannot be "the test." The problem is that the

---

[1] *Erie* ended the days of *general* federal common law. It did not end all federal common law. There are still areas in which federal courts are free to make up common law rules. But they do not include the general doctrines by which we live our daily lives. Instead, federal common law applies in interstitial areas of federal interest. For example, admiralty law and the law of international relations are governed by federal common law.

Court has used several "tests" in trying to determine when federal courts are required to apply state law (common law or statutory) in diversity cases. The three main tests come from three famous cases. No one is quite sure how these three tests are to be balanced—or, indeed, if they are all alive today. As suggested, get an idea of what your professor thinks of these.

B. A Variety of Tests

We will deal with the three major approaches as examples.

Example 1: Under state law, a case would be barred by the statute of limitations. In a diversity case, the federal judge wants to ignore the state statute of limitations and let P's case proceed. Can the judge ignore the state law?

This is *Guaranty Trust Co. v. York*, 326 U.S. 99 (1945), in which the Court held that state law governs. It gave us the "outcome determination" test, which requires the judge to ask: if I ignore state law on this point, will it lead to a different outcome in federal and state courts? If the answer is yes, the federal judge should follow state law. On the facts of *Guaranty Trust*, if we ignore the state law (statute of limitations), the case will proceed. If we apply the state law, the case will be dismissed. Those are different results. So statute of limitations is "outcome determinative," and we should follow state law. Stated another (and an unhelpful) way, statute of limitations is "substantive."

Guaranty Trust has never been overruled, though it may have been modified (see Example 3). It worked well enough on the facts of the case, but can be applied in an overly wooden way. At some point *any* rule—even something as inconsequential as whether pleadings should be on 11-inch or 14-inch paper—will be "outcome determinative." That is, if you try to file a complaint on the wrong-sized paper, the clerk will not file it and the case will not proceed. Yet it would be silly to say that a federal court should be required to follow state law on such a trivial point.

> Example 2: Under state law, an employee cannot sue her
> employer.[2] P sues Company 1, for which he did not
> work, seeking damages for personal injuries suffered
> while working for Company 2. The relationship between
> Company 1 and Company 2 opens an argument that P is a
> "statutory employee" of Company 1. If so, his case must
> be dismissed. The question is who will decide whether P
> is a "statutory employee"—the judge or a jury? State law
> says that the judge decides this question, though the
> case law on point fails to provide a reason for the rule.
> In a diversity case, can the federal judge ignore the
> state law and have a jury decide the question?

This is *Byrd v. Blue Ridge Rural Elec. Coop., Inc.*, 356 U.S. 525 (1958), in which the Court held that the federal judge could ignore state law. I, for one, think *Byrd* is the best *Erie* decision ever, because it gives us an overall approach. Most professors probably do not agree, however, and, at any rate, the Court has not done much with *Byrd* in the intervening decades. The Court explained that the Tenth Amendment commands federal courts to apply state substantive law and topics "bound up" with substantive law. (Problem: the Court has never defined "bound up." It would seem to include things like burdens of proof—they do not define when one side is liable to another, but are pretty close, because they tell us who would have to prove what.)

In *Byrd*, the question (whether the judge or jury should decide whether P is a "statutory employee") was neither

---

[2] This is ubiquitous. In every state, claims by injured employees against employers are subject to workers' compensation laws, under which the employees receive specified benefits without having to show fault.

substantive nor bound up. That meant it was a matter of "form and mode." On these matters, the federal court should assess whether it is outcome determinative (under *Guaranty Trust*). If it is, the federal court should apply state law *unless some federal interest outweighs the state interest.* In matters of form and mode, then, the Tenth Amendment does not apply, so the application of state law is not compelled. But policy counsels the federal court to follow state law on outcome-determinative matters of form and mode. In *Byrd*, the Court found that the federal courts, as an independent system for the administration of justice, have an interest in allocating authority between judge and jury. In contrast, the state had no reason for its rule, so the state interest was not weighty. Thus, the federal court could have a jury decide whether P was a "statutory employee."

> Example 3: Under Federal Rule 4, substituted service of process (Chapter 2, § F) would be proper on the facts of the case. Under state law, substituted service of process is not permitted. In a diversity case, must the federal court follow state law? Surely, the question is "outcome determinative" in the *Guaranty Trust* sense: if we apply state law, the case is dismissed, and if we do not, the case continues.

This is *Hanna v. Plumer*, 380 U.S. 460 (1965), in which the Court held that state law was irrelevant. Read *Hanna* carefully. The Court did two things. First, it shifted the focus of the "outcome determination" analysis. The method of serving process is outcome-determinative in the *Guaranty Trust* sense—if we apply state law, the case is dismissed, but if we ignore state law, the case continues. But in *Hanna* the Court said that the difference between applying state law (on the one hand) and ignoring state law (on the other) should be assessed in accordance with the "twin aims of *Erie*" (a phrase not used before). The twin aims are to avoid (1) forum shopping and (2) the inequitable administration of the law. Under this view, the federal judge asks: if I ignore state law on this issue, will it cause litigants to flock to federal court (if they can invoke subject matter jurisdiction)? If so, that's bad because it is automatically unfair. Why? Because you can only avoid state law by going to federal court, and instate plaintiffs cannot go to federal court because they cannot invoke diversity.

Hanna seems to modify *Guaranty Trust* with the twin aims test. Oddly, it did not expressly overrule *Guaranty Trust*, however, and a remarkable number of lower courts still use the old-fashioned *Guaranty Trust* analysis. Still, a lot of professors think the wooden approach of *Guaranty Trust* is no longer part of the law. Some other professors, however, conclude that you should apply both the wooden *Guaranty Trust* test and the twin aim approach. (Get a sense of what your professor thinks.)

The second thing *Hanna* did, however, was truly extraordinary: it told us that what it just said about "twin aims" did not apply anyway, because *Hanna* did not present an *Erie* issue at all!

C. Two Doctrines, Not One

Hanna established that there is a preliminary step before we even get to *Erie*. We will call it the *Hanna* step, and it requires the federal judge to ask: is there a federal directive on-point that covers the issue that I must decide? If so, the federal court must apply the federal directive, so long as it is valid. There is no *Erie* analysis. There is no outcome-determination or *Byrd* balancing of interests or "twin aims" of *Erie*. Under the supremacy clause of the Constitution, an applicable, valid federal directive trumps state law. The federal directive may be the Constitution, a federal statute, or a Federal Rule of Civil Procedure.

This is why the language about "twin aims" in *Hanna*, which is a gloss on the *Erie* analysis, was actually irrelevant to the holding in *Hanna*. It was dictum. In *Hanna*, there was a federal directive (Rule 4) on-point, covering the issue that the federal judge was addressing. Because Rule 4 was valid, it trumped the contrary state law.

How do we know if a federal directive is valid? Constitutional provisions are automatically valid. Federal statutes are valid if they fall within Congress's power to legislate under Article I of the Constitution, which you will study in Constitutional Law. What about a Federal Rule Civil Procedure? It is valid if it satisfies the Rules Enabling Act (REA), 28 U.S.C. § 2072, which provides that the Rules "shall not abridge, enlarge or modify any substantive right."

In *Shady Grove Orthopedic Assn., P.A. v. Allstate Ins. Co.*, 559 U.S. 393 (2010), four justices concluded that the REA is satisfied if the Rule in question can be characterized as "arguably procedural." This is not tough to meet—after all, these are the Federal Rules of Civil *Procedure*, so it is not a stretch to think the provision might be arguably *procedural*. (The Court has never held a Rule invalid.) One other justice concluded, however, that a court must look to the competing state-law provision to see whether the Federal Rule impinges on what the state was trying to accomplish. In the end, all five of these justices agreed that Rule 23—the class action rule—was valid under the REA.

After *Hanna*, then, we have a two-step approach. First, we apply *Hanna*: if there is a federal provision on point, that directly clashes with state law, the federal court applies the federal provision if it is valid. There is no *Erie* analysis. Second, if there is no federal provision on point, the federal court undertakes the *Erie* analysis to determine whether the court must apply state law (or is free to ignore state law). The trouble is that the *Erie* analysis is not clear. We have to do our best to make sense of *Guaranty*

Trust, *Byrd*, and the "twin aims" dictum from *Hanna* (even though it was dictum in *Hanna*, the Court has since applied it in *Erie* cases). If your professor has an approach, follow it. If she does not, however, it seems reasonable to apply all three of those approaches and come to a reasonable conclusion.

D. Two Illustrative Hypos

> <u>Example</u>: Federal Rule 23 permits a class action on the facts of our case. State law, however, prohibits class litigation of this particular substantive claim. In a diversity case, plaintiffs seek certification of a class under Rule 23.

Do not jump to outcome determination or twin aims or even *Erie*. The first question is whether there is a federal directive on point that directly conflicts with state law. The answer here is yes—Rule 23 is on point. This is *Shady Grove*, in which the Court held that Rule 23 applies. And, as noted above, the majority of five justices concluded that the Rule is valid under the REA. So it displaces state law in diversity cases.

> <u>Example</u>: The legislature of State X is concerned that medical costs are too high, and that one reason is excessive malpractice litigation. It passes a law that requires medical malpractice cases to be arbitrated. Arbitration is an alternative to court litigation, with no jury and limited discovery. The statute provides that an arbitration panel of three doctors and lawyers will hear the malpractice case and render a decision. (Plaintiffs do not like this, because of a widespread sense that juries award higher damages than such arbitration panels.) After the arbitration, the plaintiff has the right to go through the regular litigation stream, including jury trial—though the jury will be informed of the

arbitration decision. (Plaintiffs do not like this, because they feel the jury verdict will be reduced by the arbitration decision.) A citizen of State Y visits state X and goes to a doctor. She claims that the doctor committee malpractice, and sues in federal court in State X, invoking diversity jurisdiction. The doctor claims that the federal court in State X must send the case to arbitration under the state statute. What result?

First, is there a federal directive on-point? No. There is nothing in the Federal Rules about medical malpractice. So *Hanna* does not apply. Second, apply *Erie*, which means (unless your prof gives you a different method) accounting for the three tests discussed in § B. Here goes:

One, is the state law "outcome-determinative" under *Guaranty Trust*? Probably not. We have a sense that arbitration will result in a smaller verdict, but there is no reason to think the outcome will be different as it was in *Guaranty Trust*. After all, the plaintiff has a right to go to jury trial after the arbitration.

Two, what about *Byrd*? Well, an arbitration statute does not seem "bound up" with substantive law. It has nothing to do with what elements the plaintiff must establish. It just affects who decides whether she did establish her claim. So the state law seems to "form and mode." Even if it were outcome-determinative, is there a federal interest that outweighs the state interest? Well, there is a federal interest in jury trials, but the state law does not rob the plaintiff of a jury—it just delays jury trial. And here, unlike in *Byrd*, the state has a considerable interest in its law—it wants to reduce medical costs. That's important.

Three, what about the "twin aims?" If the federal judge ignores this state law, it will cause every plaintiff who could do so to go to federal court. (Every plaintiff will want to avoid arbitration and go to a jury directly.) This, in turn, leads to the inequitable administration of law, because citizens of State X cannot go to federal court. When they sue a State X doctor, they cannot invoke diversity, so they will be stuck in state court and stuck with the arbitration statute. So, to avoid forum shopping and this unfairness to the good people of State X, the federal judge should follow state law.

Are we sure this is answer is "right?" No. But we have discussed all the relevant factors and come to a reasonable conclusion. In an amorphous topic like *Erie* (as in personal jurisdiction), that is all we as law students and lawyers can be expected to do!

Table of Cases

Anderson v. Liberty
Lobby, Inc. 105
Asahi Metal Industry Co.,
Ltd. v. Superior Court of
California......................... 29
Ashcroft v. Iqbal................. 87
Atlantic Marine Construction
Company, Inc. v. U.S.
District Court 82
Bell Atlantic Corporation
v. Twombly 87
Burger King Corporation
v. Rudzewicz.................... 27
Burnham v. Superior
Court of California 33
Byrd v. Blue Ridge Rural
Electric Cooperative,
Inc. 161
Calder v. Jones................... 32
Celotex Corporation v.
Catrett 105
Cohen v. Beneficial
Industrial Loan
Corporation.................... 121
Daimler AG v. Bauman 35
Erie Railroad Co. v.
Tompkins....................... 157
Exxon Mobil Corporation
v. Allapattah Services,
Inc. 143
Feathers v. McLucas........... 39
Goldlawr, Inc. v. Heiman ... 81
Goodyear Dunlop Tires
Operations, S.A. v.
Brown 34
Grable & Sons Metal
Products, Inc. v. Darue
Engineering &
Manufacturing................. 64
Gray v. American Radiator
& Standard Sanitary
Corporation..................... 39
Guaranty Trust Co. of
New York v. York 160
Hanna v. Plumer............... 162
Hanson v. Denckla............. 26
Helicopteros Nacionales de
Colombia, S.A. v. Hall..... 34
Hertz Corp. v. Friend......... 59
Hess v. Pawloski 23
Hoffman v. Blaski 81

International Shoe Co.
v. Washington 24
J. McIntyre Machinery
Ltd. v. Nicastro 30
John Swift v. George W.
Tyson 158
Louisville & Nashville
Railroad Company v.
Mottley 63
Matsushita Electric
Industrial Co., Ltd.
v. Zenith Radio
Corporation 105
McGee v. International
Life Insurance
Company 25
Milliken v. Meyer 25
Mullane v. Central
Hanover Bank &
Trust Co......................... 48
Parklane Hosiery
Company, Inc. v.
Shore............................. 156
Pennoyer v. Neff................. 21
Perkins v. Benguet
Consolidated Mining
Co.................................. 34
Scott v. Harris 104
Shady Grove Orthopedic
Associates, P.A. v.
Allstate Insurance
Co.................................. 164
Shaffer v. Heitner.............. 34
Strawbridge v. Curtiss 55
United Mine Workers of
America v. Gibbs............. 65
Van Dusen v. Barrack 82
Walden v. Fiore 32
Wal-Mart Stores, Inc.
v. Dukes........................ 140
World-Wide Volkswagen
Corporation v.
Woodson 26
Zahn v. International
Paper Company............. 143